LIFE IN LETHINNIS

LIFE IN LETHINNIS
A croft in the Highlands

RORY PUTMAN

DRAWINGS BY CATHERINE PUTMAN

Whittles Publishing

Published by
Whittles Publishing,
Dunbeath,
Caithness KW6 6EG,
Scotland, UK

www.whittlespublishing.com

© 2023 Rory Putman

ISBN 978-184995-552-2

Cover image by Brian Mullins

Printed in the UK by

CONTENTS

PREFACE

Some 30 years ago I gave up my job as a researcher and lecturer at the University of Southampton and moved with my first wife Morag to a croft at the edge of a small and remote village in the Western Highlands. This was no romantic and idealistic aspiration for the Good Life, nor really an attempt to 'get away from it all'; rather a growing disaffection with living in the overpopulated and materialistic south of England and a desire to return to our Scottish roots (both Morag and myself were half-Scots by parentage and had spent much of our early lives in Scotland). Moving to Lochuisge was like stepping back 50 years in time: most of the other residents of this tiny hamlet had been born and bred there, the majority were Gaelic-speaking and, with few of the conventional 'services', there was a strong sense of community that we had missed so greatly in the south.

This book offers a collection of memories of those first few years as we moved into and settled in our remote smallholding. Through these stories I try to capture something of the atmosphere of this remote village in the Highlands and the characters who lived there and became part of our everyday life. Since I am myself a professional biologist, and since its wildlife are themselves an essential part of living somewhere like Lochuisge, the characters featured are both human and animal as I try to give a flavour of living and working in this tight-knit community into which we were so immediately and warmly welcomed.

All the people and events described in this book are real, although places have been disguised to some extent, to protect their identity, and some names have been changed (to protect me from lawsuits from those still living!). Enough clues remain that professional biologists or those with a keen interest in natural history will readily identify the peninsula, while those personalities included will readily recognise themselves: I trust I have included nothing to offend them.

I thank Keith Whittles of Whittles Publishing for having the courage to support me in a departure from my normal sort of writing and again owe enormous thanks to my editor, wordsmith Caroline Petherick, who has once more helped improve the text with her unfailingly constructive suggestions. I have indeed appropriated her name to disguise one of my characters.

The book is dedicated to my wife Catherine, who joined me in Lochuisge in 1998 and whose illustrations enhance the text; sadly, she died before she saw the completed project in print.

Rory Putman, Banavie, June 2022

IT'S A SMALL WORLD, MY MASTERS

I sat at my desk at the university as the final weeks flew to my departure, and lifted the phone.

'A caller from the local wildlife trust who is hoping to put some radiotelemetry collars on otters in a re-introduction project,' explained Enid, my secretary, 'and wants to know if he can register the project as affiliated with your research group so that he can come under the umbrella of your Home Office licence to trap and tag.'

Carefully I explained to the caller that while some years ago I would have been only too happy to have explored such a collaboration, I was shortly leaving my position as head of the university's wildlife research unit to move to Scotland, and thus would be unable to help.

'Oh,' returned the enthusiastic caller, with apparent interest; 'whereabouts are you going?'

From this point on the conversation took a trip into the surreal. There cannot be many places left in Europe where the full electoral roll is 22 eligible adults. Lochuisge[1] is a small hamlet on the West Coast of Scotland jutting out into the Atlantic at the end of 42 miles of single-track road. Even to access the beginning of that 42-mile journey one first has to take a ferry crossing. The nearest village of any significance is 12 miles and 20 minutes back along the main road, and has a population of around 300. It is by most people's definition a remote place (although after I'd lived there for a while I heard an

---

1 Loch-*ooshke*

irritated neighbour, exasperated beyond bearing of hearing endlessly from others how remote they considered our home, retort to some Glaswegian holidaymaker that to us Glasgow was just as remote). When my wife and I first moved there, a good proportion of the population were native Gaelic-speakers, and indeed some had never been as far as that remote Glasgow.

'A small village up on the West Coast,' I replied to my unknown caller.

He persisted: 'But where?'

'You probably won't have heard of it,' I explained. 'It's on the Lethinnis peninsula and near a small village called Kinlochbuidhe.'

Unbelievably, he repeated: 'Yes, but *where*?'

Puzzled, but in order to close this curious conversation for good, I responded: 'Well, it's a little village called Lochuisge.'

'But where *IN* Lochuisge?' came the astonishing response. 'I've just built a house there.'

This bizarre coincidence was to be repeated in one form or another, over and over again, in the weeks and years which followed. Despite its size and despite its remoteness – a combination which should have conspired to give the place a low profile – it appeared in some ways the epicentre of the civilised world: everybody seemed to have been there or have some connection with the place.

Some weeks later I chanced, on a trip to Reading, to bump into an old colleague from a government research establishment, the Institute of Terrestrial Ecology. Ray was a gifted field biologist who had given up a career as a distilleries inspector to become a wildlife ecologist for the then 'Department'.[2]

The conversation took the by now familiar turn. 'I hear you're retiring back up to Scotland,' he offered. 'Whereabouts are you going?' 'Oh … an excellent place! Hans Kruuk and I worked there on a project investigating predation on lambs by hill foxes in the 1960s; the Laird then was a wonderful old character called Alice Outhwaite; Hans and I loved her.'

I later heard more of this same story from Dolina, Miss Outhwaite's housemaid of the time. With a chuckle she recalled Hans and Ray's

---

2 the Department of Agriculture for Scotland

first interview with Miss O – a redoubtable spinster who had bought the Lochuisge Estate and had farming interests not only there but across the water on the nearby island of Scarpay. A formidable lady, if somewhat deaf and affecting a large and old-fashioned Victorian ear-trumpet, Miss Outhwaite had summonsed the two young researchers into her sitting room and dispatched Dolina to fetch glasses and a decanter of whisky to welcome her guests.

Now, as perhaps one of the perks or casualties of his former profession as an inspector of distilleries, Raymond was a seasoned drinker. (Ray's idea of 'drying out' was a bottle of Scotch whisky a day; 'laying waste' involved significantly increased quantities of the water of life interrupted only by copious cans of Special Brew. In fairness, and despite his remarkable capacity, I never saw him drunk.) Ignorant of this history, Miss O imperiously tasked Ray with pouring each of them a drink; out of a natural reticence and politeness (he was after all pouring from someone else's bottle), Ray apparently splashed a generous but appropriate measure into each of the large cut-glass tumblers arranged on the side table, courteously taking one of the glasses over to Miss Outhwaite's chair. She peered at her half-full tumbler suspiciously before barking: 'Young man. What is wrong with the top half of the glass?'

Perhaps Lochuisge was simply a Mecca for biologists (or drinkers)? Certainly the area is a botanist's paradise, with orchids galore – drifts of early purple or marsh orchids, fragrant orchis, greater and lesser butterfly orchids, bee orchid, Irish lady's tresses, twayblade, globe-flower; the list is endless, with as many as five species of orchid in flower within a single square metre of turf. With a very low human population, Lochuisge is also incredibly undisturbed and a haven for otters, wildcat, pine martens, eagles and other wildlife. So it is indeed an interesting place for a biologist, and many of its regular visitors were undeniably keen naturalists who had independently 'discovered' this wildlife haven.

But Lochuisge's knack of coincidence reaches far further. I had been living in my house, Allt na Mhuillin, for perhaps ten years when a stranger appeared at the door: 'We have just taken the tenancy of the

Mains,[3] and the Laird [by that time Miss Outhwaite's nephew, Hector Maclean] has told us we should come and introduce ourselves – partly simply as new neighbours, but also because like you, we have livestock and intend to run the place as a smallholding or croft. My name is John Petherick. That's P-E-T—'

'Oh yes,' I interrupted, 'Fitzharry's Road in Abingdon. We used to be neighbours then, too.' Remarkably, 40 years ago John and I had as children lived next-door-but-one in a housing estate 500 miles away to the south. I had left when I was nine; John would have been about eleven. We had not clapped eyes on each other since, yet here we were 40 years later and 500 miles away, both crofting in a remote West Coast village of 22 souls.

And yet, I myself had acquired the place almost by accident, although certainly not on a whim.

After many years working as a lecturer and research biologist in the university system, I had grown somewhat disenchanted with the way the politics of further education seemed to be developing – and indeed with the growing materialism of the south in general, where what seemed to matter most was job title and thus social status and earnings. Genuinely saddened by the changes and by what I felt was being lost in terms of a world where people mattered for who, and not what, they were, I determined to escape and move back to the world I had known through my grandparents: a world with a strong sense of community and where people cared.

This decision was not taken easily: I was at that time only in my early forties and inevitably would have to make my living in the future self-employed. Many of my colleagues (burdened, as we were not, with children and mortgages) thought we were incredibly courageous to wade so far out into the unknown, but this was not the classic naïve 'return to our roots' of a disillusioned townie looking to escape to the Good Life, or the pipedream of an idealist based upon too-extensive reading of Lillian Beckwith's Hebridean idyll. Both Morag and I were of mixed parentage: Scots, tainted with English; we both loved the West Coast. I had lived most of my life in country villages, and all the time

---

3 Scottish term for the farmstead associated with a private Estate, originally managed in-hand.

we had been married we had managed and maintained a smallholding wherever we had lived, so that we knew better than many what we were taking on and that we would at least survive.

I have lost count of the number of properties we reviewed and rejected over a search which lasted nearly five years. Part-way through that seemingly endless search, we spotted in the local Highland newspaper an advertisement for a house and garden ground in a little village called Lochuisge in Lethinnis. We had never actually been there, although on a previous occasion – returning from a visit to view some near-derelict croft-house at Diabaig in Torridon – I had nearly got as far as Lochuisge, turning back some 5 or 6 miles short due to lack of time (and a growing lack of daylight). But all that was offered with that house was less than one acre and thus at the time we ignored it, since we still had our minds set on somewhere with more potential for our existing livestock. Six months later we idly noticed that it was advertised again; seeing that it was still on the market my wife persuaded me we should at least look at it – and since it was being sold off from a larger Estate, enquire if perhaps some more land might be released with it. This time we did persevere to the end of the road, and I immediately fell in love with the house and the whole peninsula. Despite my repeated requests, however, the selling agents were adamant that no additional land would be available. I pointed out that clearly no one had offered on the property so far in over six months of advertising, since it was still on the market – but to no avail.

In desperation I challenged them: 'Have you even taken this suggestion back to the vendor? Have you even *asked* him?' It was apparent that they had not; that evening I received a phone call from the Laird asking exactly what extra land we required and why we wanted it. I explained about our current lifestyle and that we wanted space for our chickens, our herd of dairy goats (by that time we were milking nine), some sheep, and space for a market garden. This was followed by a long silence.

In a flash of inspiration my wife prompted me, sotto voce: 'Tell him that we're not property developers: we don't see it as a building plot. Tell him that we'll sign something undertaking we will never build on it and if we ever sell we'll sell it back to the Estate.'

A stroke of pure brilliance. At once the Laird replied: 'Oh that's very good, that'll be fine then.' And when I enquired delicately about the implications for the cost he said, 'No, no, that's fine; we'll simply include that within the existing price.' We were not about to haggle.

The move was a nightmare over which we should perhaps draw a veil. Friends fortunately offered to take holiday and help us transport the livestock overnight in a veritable flotilla of Land Rovers and stock trailers; all but one unfortunate chicken survived the 500-mile journey unscathed. Packing up our thatched New Forest home was another matter, and in the end two of Pickfords' largest removal vans appeared in the driveway. The first vehicle was swiftly loaded to about three-quarters full and then the removal men began on the second. When I enquired why, I was told that this was why we had to have two vans: not so much for volume as because of weight restrictions. The remainder of the house contents made small impression on the cavernous interior of the second lorry and the men were looking slightly uncertain about the need for two vehicles after all. So we started loading the farm equipment and the accoutrements for the animals, emptying shed after shed until there was a more satisfactory fill to the second van. Somewhat to their surprise I reappeared with lengths of timber, old planking, all the ironmongery and 'mathoms' I knew after years of near self-sufficiency were too precious to leave behind and yet which the removal men clearly thought was simply a load of old junk; it was not long at all before we had not only completely filled the second removal van, but increased substantially the fullness of the first … But at last all was inside and the doors were closed.

'Right,' said the foreman, 'we'd better be off if we're going to get this unloaded and back home again tonight.'

Registering this last in some alarm, I asked 'Do you actually know where we're going?' 'Oh, somewhere in Scotland,' he returned – clearly with the general Anglocentric ignorance of the geography of anything north of Watford and the usual southerner's perception that the country gets progressively smaller as one moves further north so that Scotland is in effect only a small protuberance on the top of England.

'Ah,' I said, fetching a map and pointing to our destination, while explaining also about single-track roads and the need for taking a ferry; 'there's no way you're going to do it in two days, let alone one.'

There was a stunned silence and a significant reappraisal. The foreman smiled weakly and said: 'Do you mind if I go and phone my wife?'

But they got there (even if the ferry crew did have to remove the safety rails from the ferry ramp to get these giant pantechnicons on board, one at a time, and with admirable restraint forbore from drawing attention to the weight restriction signs). Driving through the night, we ourselves had beaten them to it and with help from many of our new neighbours-to-be, we unloaded in almost record time.

'Blimey,' offered one of the Pickford's drivers, looking around him at the somewhat empty, if breathtakingly beautiful, landscape; 'I see now why you wanted all that 'junk'. Looks like you might need it after all!' (A completely accurate prediction in that almost all that same 'junk' had been used up in one project or another within two years or so, and subsequently I had to take the extreme step of *buying* screws and nails and hinges – a novel and rather humbling experience for someone who has always reused and repurposed.)

The other simply smiled weakly once more and said 'Where's the nearest pub?'

When we explained that it was 42 miles back, at the ferry, he blanched visibly and hastened to start his engine, leaving us happy but surrounded by rather a large quantity of packing crates and furniture. Fortunately it was not raining, so we left it there and went to talk to the goats in their spacious new accommodation.

LIVING WITH LEAKS

When we had taken over Allt na Mhuillin, Lochuisge was still a village composed almost entirely of those who had been born and brought up there. Alastair, the husband of the postmistress, was an incomer (he had been born at the ferry port, some 40 miles away and had only lived in Lochuisge for 50 years) but there were only two houses actually sold away as holiday homes, and the rest of the residents lived a life almost unchanged since the disruption of Alastair's arrival 50 years before. Gaelic-speaking Lochuisge, with the arrival of the weekly baker's van the highlight of the working week, was like stepping back a generation in time – and a village totally apart from the comparative bustle of its larger neighbour, Kinlochbuidhe, 12 miles back down the road. Indeed, the two communities were almost completely separated, and they rarely interacted.

In part this separation was historical; in the days before motor transport, 12 miles' separation was a considerable distance and there would have been little interaction. As most commerce and trade was by boat, both villages had closer contacts with neighbouring hamlets across the water on Scarpay than with each other; even in the 1960s Miss Outhwaite commuted between her Estates of Lochuisge and her lands on Scarpay by Estate boat rather than travel by car. In addition the ancestral lairds of Lochuisge were Catholic, and while many of their villagers were Presbyterian, the villages remained in separate parishes – a distinction clearly marked at the parish boundary, where funeral processions would pause, rest the coffin of the deceased and change pall-bearers for the final journey once across the parish line. A small cairn would be built to commemorate the resting place of each coffin before its onward journey, and there is to this day a Lilliputian village of small cairns on the parish boundary.

But in part the distinction was also cultural: Lochuisge had grown up as crofting village in the feu[4] of the great Estate, and most of the residents of the tiny hamlet had had employment on the Estate itself. Some of the residents of Kinlochbuidhe also worked on their local Estate as shepherds or gardeners or handymen, but Kinlochbuidhe was altogether a more cosmopolitan place and also boasted employment in 'the Forestry'[5] or in the local quarry. There was a shop and a social club and even a hotel, and Andy-the-Van did not bother to stop at Kinlochbuidhe on his weekly pilgrimage to Lochuisge. All it took was 12 miles of distance, and the two settlements were worlds apart – and in truth it was hard to say which looked down more upon the other.

When we arrived, Morag and I were, as I note, the first real incomers (other than Alastair-the-Post) to take up residence in the village. Doubtless we were viewed with some suspicion, although we were made to feel very welcome; and when it became clear that we had no wish to try and change the place – as many 'white settlers' seem determined to do – and that indeed we lived a crofting lifestyle much akin to their own, any initial suspicions were quickly dissipated. My drying-fence for hay attracted initial surprise,[6] but when, after a good mackerel run, I slung a section of old trawl net over the corrugated-iron roof of the byre and hooked the surplus catch through the meshes by the gills to dry, we had clearly 'made it'. With tears in their eyes (I suspect to this day that they may have been tears of laughter rather than nostalgia) our neighbours exclaimed that **this** was a thing they had not seen since their own parents' days.

Sheep they were accustomed to, and chickens; and while the

---

4 a Scots legal arrangement consisting of a lease on a fixed rent
5 commercial plantations largely managed by the Forestry Commission
6 a structure copied from small farms scattered around the coast in Iceland, whereby a temporary or more permanent fenceline of wooden posts and line-wires is erected, over which one can then drape swatches of cut grass to dry in the sun and sea breezes

geese and the goats may have been viewed as slight eccentricity, our reclamation of the old walled vegetable garden assured our near-self-sufficiency and assured our neighbours that we were no fly-by-nights or naïve city-dwellers simply aspiring to some ideological 'simple life' but were relatively practical country folk not so different from themselves. Allt na Mhuillin had in any event lain empty for some years before we bought it, and to be truthful, many told us how nice it was of an evening to see lights again from the old house. Seonaid, the postmistress, remarked with full sincerity that they all realised in any case that if they did not welcome and embrace newcomers the village would die on its feet, since most of the existing native residents were elderly (at 42, I was the youngest by 20 years) and there was no new generation of natives to keep the village alive. Unfortunately, such logic, however valid, might in practice amount to little more than a formal post-hoc rationalisation to appease their own sensitivities about invasion by outsiders, and certainly would not by itself ensure a genuine welcome; Lochuisge however did make us truly welcome.

The property we had bought from Alice Outhwaite's nephew was a former lodge house and its associated croftland on the edge of the Lochuisge Estate: the boundary property on the margin of the Estate, named in Gaelic for the nearby mill-stream, Allt na Mhuillin (Alt na Voulin). Before it had been bought into the Estate itself, the property had been an old inn – a staging post for travellers along the tortuous coast road to the statutory ferry crossing between Lethinnis and Ardnamurchan – and perhaps one of the only survivors of the reprisals against the Jacobites at the end of the 1745 uprising. The main landowners in the peninsula and their crofting tenants were largely Catholic, and in punishment for its allegiance to the bonnie prince the land was torched at the orders of the Duke of Cumberland and burnt from end to end – fire that could be seen for many, many miles, to serve as a dire warning. Local tradition however has it that as an independent freehold, not in feu to a Catholic landlord, the inn itself was spared.

A century or so later the property had been annexed to the Lochuisge Estate; the house was refurbished and then extended for occupation by the Gordon owners of the Estate – still Catholics – when the main Estate house had once more been damaged in a subsequent fire. Lady Gordon evicted her shepherd, took over the house and extended it, doubling its size, as well as installing gracious windows, plaster moulding and all the other accoutrements of a civilised life. She had also built a byre and, at some distance from the house itself, a laundry. Fortunately there had not been too much attempt at modernisation over the intervening years; some subsequent occupant, less appreciative of Lady Gordon's stylistic choices, had installed in the main sitting room an ugly 1950s fireplace (inset with pebbles collected from the beach, painted bright colours in glaring enamel) as well as painting one end wall a hideous orange, but apart from that the integrity of the original structure had not been too badly attacked.

The house and policies[7] I had acquired matched almost exactly the original boundaries of the old inn. The byre, which stood at the top of an incline sloping up behind the house, had clearly originally been a carriage-shed and stabling – presumably accommodation for the horses of travellers stopping over at the inn before travelling on to the ferry at Shieldaig. A curious single-roomed hovel at the top of a flight of stone steps at the rear of the house, unheated and almost like a prison cell with its raw stone walls and floor, was accessed by its own door and not in any way connected with the rest of the building; this apparently had been where the ostlers would have slept. At the rear of the house itself (the remains of the original inn) were three small bedrooms upstairs, while downstairs was a small dining room and a bar. At least we were told it had served this function, and there were indeed sockets in both lintel and stone sill of the window which were understood in the past to have held steel bars for added security of the alcohol store within.

Before her occupation, Lady Gordon had added almost a mirror image to the front of the house, but in much grander style: a fine morning room with an old-fashioned range, and the high-ceilinged sitting room of the vile fireplace and orange walls, as well as kitchens and utility rooms. At some point someone had installed an inside bathroom upstairs between the two sizeable main bedrooms. In her time, clearly, the rear part of the house had been adapted for servants –

---

7 grounds

and we were to hear many a tale of local swains escaping through the sash windows of the dining room when interrupted in their devotions; more than one lady's maid in service to the Gordons or their visitors married a local boy and stayed behind when the visiting gentry left.

As part of the renovations Lady Gordon had also created a fine walled garden, although by our time this had fallen into gross neglect and was marked only by the persistent rhubarb (which to me always seems to survive any number of years of abandonment; flourishing rhubarb stools have emerged from hiding in every old garden I have tried to reclaim). She – or someone – had also planted a pair of magnificent false cypress,[8] sculpted by the salt and the sea-winds into the most curious shapes, but tall and grand – and known to all locally as Lochuisge's Policemen; certainly we had no other constabulary.

Allt na Mhuillin had however been empty for many years. The slate roof on the old laundry had long since fallen in; the back wall of the carriage-shed-byre had collapsed, and the tin-roofed single-storey building known as the Bothy (erected as summer accommodation for guests rather than as some small gazebo: fully panelled and containing two bedrooms and a small bathroom), was also far from its original splendour. Apart from the 1950s excrescence of the sitting room fireplace (quickly ripped away to expose the original fireplace behind, in which we installed a large woodburner), the front of the house itself was not in bad condition, but the rear had suffered from rotted rooflights allowing in copious quantities of West Coast rain; and the original lead piping in the walls had not been properly disconnected from the private water supply, but simply hammered flat and folded over. Over the years these pipes had perished or simply the folded ends had not proved as watertight as imagined, so that water had seeped into the stonework and washed away all the mortar.

A tractor axle had at some point been inserted into the wall of the rear dining room to prop up the cracked lintel of its enormous fireplace, and a free-standing brick wall erected underneath as further support. Years of seeping water had rusted the axle through, and the stub walls of bricks, never tied into the surrounding stone leant forward forlornly into the room and offered no support whatsoever. And this

---

8 *Chamaecyparis*

was the ground floor – with goodness knew how many tons of stone supported (or rather unsupported) above. Removal of that wall and the tractor axle above was one of the more nerve-wracking things I have attempted, though mercifully all went well. The same could not be said on the other side of the rear hallway, where removal of some rotting plasterwork in the far corner of the old bar, subsequently converted into a bathroom (and thus concealing even more unsealed lead piping) resulted in the total collapse of the inner wall in an avalanche of rubble. Fortunately, as it transpired, this was a wall of two layers, and the outer skin held firm as we rebuilt the inner stonework.

But others have written of the trials and tribulations of renovating old houses in remote places, whether in France or Spain,[9] the setbacks or the perils of local builders (ours was outstanding) and while, like them, we lived for many months with rubble and concrete dust, moving our possessions from room to room as the builders finished one room or required access to another, our builder was superb and our only real problems was the endless battle with deliveries and West Coast time. I began to doubt that the story was apocryphal about the old Celt who was asked if Gaelic had a word equivalent to the Spanish 'mañana' and who, after careful deliberation responded that he did not think the language possessed a word which conveyed quite the same sense of urgency …

While the house was beginning to take shape – or at least we were able to restore to it some of its former glory – we had also managed successfully to underpin the Bothy, and, using car jacks to lift the roof beams for the duration, had replaced the back wall of the old carriage-shed and converted it to a byre and milking parlour. The chickens were comfortably installed in an old stone and slate kennel block, and the goats had new wooden stalls within their refurbished carriage-shed. Each day's routine was not new – we had been keeping livestock for many years – but needed adapting to our new surroundings and the different facilities available. Not wanting to chance it with the abundant local pine martens, we built a secure hen run for the fowl. The six or so acres of flat grassland below the track, the remains of a raised beach, were fenced and divided into two paddocks, and the goats let out into

---

9 *A Year in Provence, The Olive Farm,* and *Driving Over Lemons*

one or the other paddock each fine day; inevitably, on the West Coast, not all days were fine, which is why they also required their roomy, well-strawed stalls within the byre at the top of the hill. Morning and evening milking resumed its peaceful pattern.

I have always enjoyed working with livestock, and have always found that at the end of a tiring and commonly stressful working day, to sterilise the milking pail and churns with boiling water and go out to do the evening milking helped me relax. True, you have to relax, because goats will not let down their cream-rich milk properly if they detect any tension; but it was a relaxing occupation in any case, with my head nuzzled into the warm, sweet-smelling flank and the rhythmic 'drum' of each squirt of fresh milk against the bottom of the stainless milking pail.

Those who imagine she-goats to be malodorous are mistaken; if well cared-for and mucked out scrupulously carefully every day and bedded again on clean straw, their smell is actually a wonderful warm one, mixed with that of fresh straw.

The milk, too, despite the suspicion with which it is viewed by many, carries a taint only if handled badly. It *can* pick up bad odours and an off-flavour very quickly to be sure, but if transferred straight after milking through a milk filter (to take out any hairs or flakes of skin) and then quickly chilled, it is sweet and creamy – with almost a hint of coconut milk. And weight for weight, and in relation to the quantities of food consumed, a good goat far outperforms a cow in terms of production, with a good milker capable of producing up to 2 gallons of milk a day at the peak of a lactation (which can also last, without the need for annual matings), for up to five years. Volume drops a bit over the winter, but rises again, without the need for the goat to have another kid, the following spring.

Gradually, then, we became more settled. Access from the road to the Big House was via the track which divided our own house and its garden ground from our two fenced paddocks below, but apart from the daily passage of the Estate handyman, John Angus, morning and evening, we were relatively undisturbed. The raised terrace of the paddocks dropped steeply away into a sheer rocky cliff, to the slopes of which clung hazel and oak woodlands, before encircling the bay itself.

Amongst the crevices of this cliff and in the trees themselves lived pine martens and the occasional wildcat. At its foot was an otter holt, and among the tangled seaweed of the rocky shoreline the otters foraged for crabs and small fish trapped in the rock pools. Roe deer wandered freely through the gardens, and indeed our fencing of the paddocks for the goats had to be adapted with the installation of low-level one-way gates like modified badger gates, once we had discovered that our original fencing could result in young kids[10] being trapped within the fields and separated from their mothers. As I sat during the day at my desk in the modified bar/bathroom, it was always a pleasure to watch a graceful roe doe pass the window unconcerned, or a buck stop to browse titbits from one of the flowering shrubs on the bank behind the house.

---

10 Young roe deer are kids, as against calves in red deer and fawns in the other UK deer species.

THOSE WILDER NEIGHBOURS

Wildlife indeed there was aplenty, albeit with the curious distinction that Lethinnis lacks any medium-sized mammals; by biogeographic accident, on this peninsula there are no squirrels (neither red nor grey), no rats, no rabbits and only a few mountain hares on the highest tops. (There is in fact a curious statement in the Old Statistical Account of Scotland, dating from 1791 that no rats would ever live in Lethinnis. The remark was apparently based simply on local tradition, and cited an instance when many rats had been observed coming ashore from vessels anchored along the coast but that these had disappeared again completely within a few years. My own more prosaic suspicion is that many of these medium-sized mammals may simply never have managed to colonise the peninsula through its narrow isthmus to the mainland; those which did must have had to run the gauntlet of the many predators which persist in this wild and undisturbed landscape – and perhaps had thus been unable to build up numbers sufficiently to establish a permanent presence.)

By contrast to this curious lack of medium-sized prey species, there is a surprising diversity of predators. And as a consequence of this curious lack of medium-sized prey species (whatever the cause), all the many and varied predators – the foxes, wildcats, pine martens, eagles and abundant buzzards – are actually sharing the same rather limited prey base. Indeed, as a mainstay many of the predators depended – even larger species such as buzzards and cats – on the numerous fieldmice and voles. Golden eagles soared over the hills behind the house or cruised gently on the updrafts from the sea-cliffs, often drifting directly above the goat paddocks; the eagles too had a varied diet: they certainly took voles and mice but supplemented this with feeding off carrion, or taking full advantage in season of dead lambs from the lambing fields or the grallochs[11] left on the hill during the stalking seasons. They were not above taking the occasional young roe deer or even red deer calves, and I have had first-hand reports of eagles harassing a group of red deer passing single file along a precipitous track, to swoop down and 'hood' the face of a calf with their huge wings, panicking it and temporarily blinding it so that it missed its footing and fell to the rocks below.

Martens too had a catholic diet – once again based heavily on small rodents, although for some reason the martens had a clear preference for voles and especially short-tailed field voles. But like the foxes, they also took a considerable amount of invertebrate prey – almost coming to specialise in the bumbling *Geotrupes* dung beetles through the abundant summer, to the extent that the martens' characteristic tarry droppings sparkled an iridescent violet from the skeletal remains they contained. They scavenged along the shorelines too, picking up stranded crabs and crustaceans when they could, and over the autumn gorged themselves on the abundant blackberries. Rowanberries were also taken, but these bitter fruits could only be consumed in moderation; it seemed that this restraint in consumption of rowan was something that had to be learnt, and early in the season it was not uncommon to come across piles of barely-digest rowanberries vomited up by adolescent martens yet to learn that these fruits should be not be gorged upon but consumed in moderation only.

---

11 deer intestines

It seems that, while this large, cat-sized mustelid has a very localised distribution in Scotland, where it does occur it can occur in significant densities. Regular sightings of these fierce but attractive animals with their chocolate-brown fur and pale lemon chest patch or 'bib' delighted visitors, and not a few households further supplemented their diet with bread-and-strawberry-jam sandwiches (an especial favourite) on outside – or even inside – feeding tables.

Indeed, it was this addiction to strawberry jam (and even more especially fresh hens' eggs) which prompted neighbours of ours (in this part of the world neighbours include anyone within a 50-mile radius) to initiate a detailed study of the martens and their social behaviour. Retired farmers from Yorkshire, they have been feeding and monitoring individual pine martens coming to their garden / house for many years, and can identify numerous individuals. From their observations and endless hours of videotape their observations begin to challenge established wisdom, in that they have a resident pair/family group regularly visiting their living room – and in addition loads of transients (seen once and never again) who will settle if there is a vacancy but otherwise are immediately challenged by the residents and move on.

According to their observations, male martens are intolerant of strange males, but tolerant of their own male offspring even after these reach maturity (or even after they return as mature adults after a period away). Female kits are driven out by the mother at one year (in preparation for her next litter) but male offspring are tolerated to remain, even by the resident male, and may form close association with the male. Most unexpectedly, these male kits from previous litters are believed by our friends to assist in rearing of the new litter, and they claim they have evidence to suggest they help train the new litter to hunt/forage/find food sources. In contrast to conventional wisdom, their observations suggest that rather than roving males simply mating with a female and moving on, adult males persist as permanent members in the family group, helping rear the kits and helping to provision the begging young. They claim that these dominant males stick around even after that and may regularly associate with their adolescent male offspring, again assisting with their 'training'.

Otters fed along the strandline too, or fished among the bladder wrack in the deeper waters beyond. While, especially, immature animals nearing independence eat a lot of crustaceans and molluscs, these are not particularly nutritious and the otters must include an adequate proportion of true fish in their diet to survive and thrive. Also, although often seen along the shoreline, they cannot live entirely by salt water; the salt clogs in their fur and compromises both streamlining and waterproofing. so that each otter must withdraw to fresh water at least once a day to groom and clean its pelage. Breeding dens are also often a long way inland, and I recall my wife's surprise and consternation soon after we had arrived, on inadvertently cornering a large bitch otter and her young cubs in a back corner of the Bothy. The otter won that particular stand-off, and my wife beat a strategic retreat.

Much of the coastline around Lochuisge was wooded, and indeed had managed to retain its original costume of coastal Atlantic oakwood with its characteristic understorey of hazel. The oaks had obviously been managed in the past, and the coast was littered with old stone charcoal-burners' kilns. In protection of the improved grazing of the lower ground and the seasonal crops of the crofts and farms which hugged the shore, a long hill fence kept the larger red deer to the hill ground, and the roe could roam these oak and hazel woodlands with little competition from their larger cousins except for the occasional animal which might swim round the end of the hill fence.

Few Estates bothered much about shooting the roe for sport either – apart, perhaps, for a very occasional buck – and it was always a source of great pleasure to see these elegant little animals picking their way delicately amongst the woodland stems or grazing out onto the uncut pastures. In the fields below the house they establish a 'play-ring', a circular ring flattened in the long grass, which develops during courtship chases as the male pursues a chosen female. Roe bucks are quite aggressive in the breeding season (which occurs in mid-summer, earlier than that of other deer species), and establish exclusive territories from which any other male is vigorously expelled.

Usually these territories are larger than the ranges of the females and thus any individual buck's territory may overlap with that of two or three females. This sounds a fairly simple mating strategy in that any male has access to adult females whose ranges his territory overlaps, but in truth the females are not so passive in this matter and when they come into oestrus may actually leave their normal range, travelling quite considerable distances on so-called 'mating excursions', sizing up potential alternative mates.

Mating involves these characteristic circular courtship chases in mid-summer – but after the eggs have been fertilised the embryo goes into a state of suspended animation and does not develop further; actual implantation into the uterus and the start of normal foetal development is delayed until December or January. This means that the kids are born in the early summer, in synchrony with those of other species and at a time when there is active growth of vegetation and thus plenty of food for the mother to support the demands of lactation. Again, unlike other species, roe commonly have twins or even triplets, although not all necessarily survive. Eagles and foxes are both keen predators of newborn roe kids, and many are lost in the first few weeks of life. Indeed some 30–40 per cent of all kids born may succumb to predation within the first two months of their lives; it always seemed a tragedy to me whenever I encountered this (or when, attracted by the piteous screaming call, to try and rescue a kid only a few days old from the jaws of a fox), but I suppose foxes have to eat – and feed their young – as well.

Above the hill fence on the wilder rocky moorlands roamed the larger red deer. Like roe deer, red deer are native to Great Britain and are actually Britain's largest land mammal, weighing up to 160 kg. Although historically a woodland species, red deer have secondarily adapted themselves to living on the bleak windswept moorlands of the Highlands, seeking shelter in the topography of the ground itself or withdrawing into deeper corries out of the line of the wind. Red deer are one of the more social species of deer, and herds may be quite mobile over an extensive shared range. Hinds tend to be more closely 'fixed' to a smaller home range of perhaps a couple of square kilometres, but stags range much more widely. Red deer are mixed feeders, with diet consisting primarily of grasses and low shrubs such as heather and blaeberry, and woody browse where it is available. Large body size confers the capacity to digest more fibrous forages, and there is even some evidence that, at least amongst moorland populations, males subsist on a diet higher in fibre and lower in nutritional value than that selected by breeding females.

Red deer were, and remain, crucial to the economy of many Highland Estates (and the rural communities that they support through employment). While initially a sport made fashionable by Queen Victoria and Prince Albert, and adopted as a result by many of the gentry, stalking of red deer on the open hill now contributes somewhere in excess of £100 million to the Scottish economy – and with much of that targeted in more remote areas where there is little other source of income. Encouraged by the fashion for stalking, numbers of red deer have been allowed to increase significantly so that in some places, roaming in large herds, they have been described as 'brown gravy' poured over the hillside; but populations in our part of the world were not at such a density that they might cause damage to the surrounding vegetation, and I confess that one of the most iconic sounds of 'wilderness' Scotland is the deep roaring call of a rutting stag defending his harem of hinds, echoing through the mist of a high corrie in the autumn breeding season.

Last but not least, wild goats lived on the rocky cliffs around the shorelines. Strictly speaking these were of course feral animals descended from domestic goats gone wild, but there were three or four distinct herds within the local area, all living within a few hundred metres of the shingle beaches and rarely penetrating far inland. It seems through much of Scotland this is the case, for the goats forage extensively along the shore, feeding on the seaweeds which perhaps supplement their diet with minerals perhaps deficient in the coarse vegetation of the peaty soils of the bulk of the hill land over which they might also range.

Earlier I mentioned that well-kept female goats do not smell; by contrast, you can always tell if you are within the home range of one of these feral herds by the unmistakable stench of billy goat.[12]

---

12 Billies regularly and frequently urinate on anything/anyone within range, including themselves – head, beard, front end generally – to maximise the spread of their powerful and penetrating odour, thus define their territory.

A PRETENSION OF PEAFOWL

In those early days the building work did occupy much of our attention. We were not in a position financially that we could have had anything much done in the way of restorations before we took up residence – and in any case I always prefer to be on hand to answer any queries arising as the work progresses. But it does mean living with a permanent mess, moving from room to room as work progresses, taking over those which are completed and decamping from others as the builders require access. In many instances work could not be confined to a single room at a time, and whole areas of the house came under attack, meaning that we ourselves were permanently tiptoeing around heaps of rubble. Undertaking any of our own work was inevitably difficult because of the disruption and the constant noise of jack-hammers, or the more alarming sound of falling masonry (which always wrenched me from my seat to investigate what might be the latest disaster) as well as the need to interrupt whatever one was doing to answer urgent questions from the builders, as each step in the process unearthed additional unforeseen problems.

In fairness, it must have been difficult for the builders, too, working round us – and tripping over dogs which regularly mounted escapes from the rooms in which we had them incarcerated. It must have been far more awkward and inefficient for them to work piecemeal like this, rather than just have the clear canvas of an empty house; but they never grumbled, and worked throughout with great patience and great good humour. Somehow they managed to give us access to the kitchen throughout, although it entailed picking our way across exposed earth solums[13] and negotiating the broken floorboards and rotten timbers below; I guess such provision ensured that they, too, could be sure of regular deliveries of cups of tea.

On better days, if I was not working away from home, I could at least escape outside and crack on with some of the work required there, restoring the old wooden Bothy, erecting kennels and coal-sheds, clearing the neglected ground from encroaching bracken and rhododendron. Bracken was always a scourge; so too were the rhododendrons. Quite what had induced Sir Harold Hillier to bring back this particular variety from the Himalaya one may always wonder – and whether or not he would have been so enthusiastic had he seen the wider consequences – but *Rhododendron ponticum* has certainly found Scotland much to its liking and has spread rapidly ('naturalised' is far too generous and kindly a word for this invasion) throughout the west. There were extensive hedges of 'ponticum' when we first came to Allt na Mhuillin, but over time we gradually cut them back before digging deep around the root ball to undermine them, and hitching the protruding stumps with chains to the poor old pickup, to rock the weakening stumps to and fro, to break any remaining roots – before finally wrenching them from each individual hole. It took weeks (and I genuinely think my back will never recover); but it was in its way satisfying work, despite the midges – and the logs, once seasoned, made excellent firewood. The bracken responded well to chemical attack, although wandering with a knapsack sprayer through dense jungles considerably taller than I am, spraying upwards to reach the fronds above head-height, was perhaps not especially healthy, and it was quite difficult to keep a straight line with visibility within each forest of ferns down to a few inches in any direction.

One of the more rewarding tasks was reclaiming the old walled garden. I cannot say 'restoring' it because there is no way that I was able to reinstate it to what it might have been. But a few gnarled apple trees still survived on the steep slopes behind the carriage-shed (which formed one wall of the whole), and on the lower slopes there remained

---

13 rammed-earth subfloors

a few straggly currant bushes and flourishing stools of rhubarb, which, as I mentioned earlier, will always persist, whatever the neglect.

The steep bank which comprised the upper part of the enclosed plot was held back by a retaining wall (which had started to crumble as more and more hazel trees, self-seeded along its top, pushed their roots deeper into its fabric). Below this a rough path ran from end to end of the garden, with edging stones bordering a comparatively flat expanse of deeper soil. At some point this had been covered with black polythene (clearly recycled from old silage wrap), presumably as an attempt to suppress the weeds and to pre-warm the soil in spring by collecting what heat there might be in the thin sun. Sadly, 'at some point' is the key phrase here, because the polythene had long perished; mice and voles had made many holes in the plastic, and luxuriant growths of ground elder and couch grass pushed up through the holes along with the ubiquitous rhubarb. I never got rid of the ground elder (nor did I ever try eating it; I have always been somewhat dubious about the claim that the Romans had introduced it as a food), but gradually – and with heaps of muck from the goat sheds maturing against one end wall – the plot became reasonably productive, to deliver our own potatoes, green vegetables and salads. Root vegetables like carrots and parsnips did very well, as did Jerusalem artichokes, but peas and beans were a non-starter because the seeds were always stolen by the abundant voles and mice before they even managed to germinate– and if we started them in seed trays the tops were always nipped off shortly after being transplanted. I did get some success with runner beans, but only by sowing each within an eight-inch collar of cut-down drainpipe pushed upright into the soil.

What finished off our vegetable garden restoration efforts, though, were the peafowl. Once the peacocks had found their way into the enclosed area of the walled gardens they finally put paid to any hope of growing vegetables (they are quite partial to bedding plants too).

Peafowl have always amused me with their sheer exotic extravagance (although I confess I have a sneaking preference for the more subtly coloured females). I had long cherished the notion of keeping peafowl, but they are noisy, they are notorious crop-robbers of grain fields – and they do decimate neighbours' gardens. They also suggest, in the keeper, delusions of grandeur (elegant peafowl strutting across baronial lawns). None of these objections, of course, held any force in Lochuisge.

As it turned out, John, one of our more distant neighbours (in this part of the world a neighbour is a neighbour even at half an hour's distance) had himself kept peafowl for many years but was now losing so many to increasing numbers of pine martens that he was considering getting rid of them for good (the peafowl, not the martens). John was a true craftsman in wood; trained as a boat-builder (and still with a bushy black beard, a piratical air and a neat gold ring in one ear-lobe), he worked now as a wood-turner and sculptor – although he still kept his hand in restoring old boats, and a current project was rebuilding one of Arthur Ransome's old sailing boats. He was a real artist (his pieces sell for hundreds of pounds in galleries in the south) and we had come to know him and his coastguard wife very well. When he mentioned that he was thinking of giving up the peafowl, they were soon transhipped to Allt na Mhuillin.

I knew that no one would see them (and could thus accuse me of affecting airs and graces beyond my station) – although of course they might be overheard. No one anywhere in the entire West Coast attempted growing grain crops – and we had no immediate neighbours; certainly none with cherished flower gardens which might be ravaged.

Naturally enough we kept them penned for a few weeks for them to accustom themselves to their new home before we let them free. In textbook style they stayed close to the house for a number of days before taking off on more and more distant voyages of discovery of their wider surroundings; but once they had done their research, a regular morning feed kept them tightly hefted to the croft and they never wandered far beyond our own fields and garden ground. But even if no one was actually able to see them, they would have been very hard to miss. They are very noisy (it is widely rumoured – though it may be an urban myth – that a distorted version of the powerful call was used to dub the calls of velociraptors for the film *Jurassic Park*), and even if the sound is muted over distance – as is the sound of bagpipes played out of doors, swelling and drifting as the wind changes – we in Lochuisge didn't have that benefit of distance. Males can in fact call at any time of year, but they call much more frequently between April and June (coinciding with the breeding season). Unfortunately, this is the time of year when nights are growing noticeably shorter, and they also call from first light so that probably everyone in Lochuisge could hear them at that time of year from around 4 a.m. But no one complained (except ourselves). And I think most were amused by yet another of our eccentricities.

Sadly, it did not take the peacocks long in their explorations to spy the vegetable plot, and while we did enjoy (at least for most months of the year) watching them strolling about the gardens – and the excitement each year as females, absent from the regular morning feeds, returned with a brood of little peachicks – we never again got to enjoy home-grown vegetables. Nevertheless, we have had the peafowl and their descendants ever since.

'INA'S MARCH TO THE MILL HOUSE

Tom Cameron had worked (as did so many) in the Forestry, but in his spare time worked a croft at Lochuisge – or technically, as it was in those days, in the neighbouring hamlet of Camas Inas. Unusually, perhaps for that time he was an owner-occupier. Crofters are legally tenants of the owner of whichever land they farm, which is usually an apportionment from one of the various major landowning Estates who have between them parcelled up much of the land of the Gàidhealtachd.[14] Technically, for true crofting tenure (and eligibility for various tax incentives or grant support), the crofter must in this way be a tenant; but some crofters buy their house outright, while others buy the land and lease it to themselves (or more commonly register the purchase in their wife's name and register a crofting lease from that wife). Tom certainly had bought for himself and his wife the Mill House – as it name suggests, formerly occupied by the local miller. The old mill, derelict now, had been built at a time when the Duke of Argyll (who in former times had owned the land right up to the boundary of the Lochuisge Estate) had erected mills throughout his land, forcing his crofters to bring their grain to be ground in his Estate mills, thus ensuring a monopoly and tightening the hold of the Estate over these bondsmen.

Many children in those days were known by patronym rather than formal surname – perhaps as much as anything because they all shared

---

14 the Gaelic-speaking parts of the Highlands

the same surname anyway – and Dolina, while formally a Cameron like all the others, was known for all her life as Dolly Tom. The main village of Camas Inas was a single row of croft-houses curving around the bay below the Mill House; a curve so perfectly maintained that the last house in the row had in itself a curious curved frontage in order to continue the line. With her older neighbour and lifelong friend, Hughina, who lived in the main terrace around the bay, Dolly would have attended the village school in Camas Inas before she left and, like her father, went to work for the Forestry. This was wartime, and many of the girls from the crofts went to work on the farms or laboured alongside the so-called DPs,[15] or prisoners of war, in the Forestry plantations – largely in support roles such as cooking or catering within the Forestry camps, but often directly involved at least in planting, if not in felling, timber. In the end Dolly left the Forestry to go into service as a maid in Clydebank on the outskirts of Glasgow – the furthest from Lochuisge she ever travelled in her entire life – and it was not long before she left the confusion of the great metropolis to return to the peace of Lethinnis, and went into service at the Big House. She never married and would have lived at home all her life, walking the two miles each day to take up her duties at the House under the firm eye of the housekeeper, Ina, before old Ina retired and Dolly herself took on the senior role of housekeeper.

These were tough times, and hard work and long hours were the norm both in service and on the croft. The peninsula was at that time a no-go area: many naval vessels were stationed in the Sound, so that access was restricted and so, even more than normal, families would have been dependent on the food that they could grow for themselves. Add to this mix the vagaries of the West Coast weather, when there are few weather windows when conditions are likely to be free of rain for long enough to make the hay, and the pressure was on indeed to make hay while the sun shone.

Dolly recalls one year when it had rained without ceasing. At last a dry spell arrived and everything was on hold to cut and save the meagre hay crop which would have to support the household's cattle through the winter. More rain was forecast, and the cut hay would

---

15 displaced persons

have to be lifted and placed in the stack; but by the time the cut hay was sufficiently dry it was a Sunday – and in those days the Sabbath was strictly observed. Even in my own childhood no money could be exchanged on a Sunday. Busy tourist car parks operated honesty boxes on that day alone; if some visitor went to purchase a Sunday newspaper, and left it in the room of their bed & breakfast, it would be discreetly removed and replaced with a bible. True, livestock had to be fed and watered, but wealthier farmers left this to their farm staff so that they would not have sinned through desecrating the Sabbath themselves (they appeared not to have felt concern about the sin visited upon the hired help).

And Dolly's family were good god-fearing folk – or perhaps feared the recriminations which might have been heaped upon them by more devout neighbours had they ventured into the fields on the Sunday. At all events Dolly and her family sat in the house and watched the hours turn by on the clock. Eventually midnight struck to mark the end of the Sabbath, and all were galvanised to rush out into the moonlight and start to gather the hay – to be stopped short in their tracks when one family member observed that while it might be midnight in this new-fangled summer time, there was yet an hour to wait before it would truly be midnight by 'God's time'. And wait they did, because no one really had developed any respect for this innovation of daylight-saving time (or as it remains known in these parts, 'daft time').

While Dolly went to work for the Forestry, Hughina worked first as post-lady and latterly as postmistress in the old post office by the Lochuisge shore. Little remains of that building now, and the post office has moved to Camas Inas, but there still remains one eating-apple tree that at the time of writing I regularly harvested every autumn. Ina's delivery round was extensive: the residents of Lochuisge and Camas Inas were scattered in isolated farms and crofts over many square miles, and all had to be traversed on foot. She must have been a hardy soul, tramping at least 20 miles a day to reach the more remote farmsteads, if they had post to deliver or collect, often walking the most direct routes over the hills with no formal paths. Only once did she admit she had been a trifle anxious, when coming around a corner in late autumn to disturb at rather closer quarters than was strictly comfortable a rutting stag, fired up by testosterone and adrenaline, who did not take kindly to the intrusion.

Ina had retired by the time I came to Lochuisge, although Dolly religiously continued to walk the two miles each day to her work at the Big House. She enjoyed being in service, and I think it had become an essential part of her personality and her actual 'being', as well as of her daily routine, for she had never married. Some feminists or social activists might consider her role as a servant in some ways demeaning but, quite to the contrary, Dolly was immensely proud of her position in the Big House; her role defined her and gave her a tremendous sense of worth and value, as well as helping to fill her otherwise lonely days. In the evenings she would visit Ina in Sealach na Mara, or more usually, Ina would walk down the hill to the Mill House for a wee strupak and a blether[16] before returning at dusk to her own home and husband Davie. As nights drew in towards the end of the year, these peregrinations would be undertaken in the half-dark or even fully after nightfall; to be sure her friend was safe on the journey, Dolly would stand at the porch of the Mill House and call, reassured by calls in return from the departing Ina. Their melodic 'coo-ees' would echo through the dusk until Ina was safe home.

The 'knack', indeed tradition, of making one's own entertainment has not left this part of the Highlands – nor had, at that time, the tradition of open-handed hospitality. You could not call at any neighbour's house in the village without being offered a cup of tea – or something stronger – and a scone or freshly battered pancake (or drop scone). To visit the post office in the hopes of purchasing a stamp was an operation to which you must expect to devote at least an hour or two while tea was drunk and news was exchanged (even if you had been there only the previous day); cattle prices at the local auction market would be discussed and closely dissected, or the state of some other unfortunate neighbour's stock-fences or his haemorrhoids. Perhaps during all of this, Niall the young tractor driver would call by and drop in; he too, probably only wanted a stamp or a postal order but would stop for a cup of tea … and remember that he had his piano accordion in the van, so he would be sent back out to collect the instrument and

---

16 cup of tea and a chat

start to play a few traditional tunes. Others passing by would stop and join in with the singing, and before you knew where you were it *was* time for a dram; and the simple purchase of a stamp begun at two in the afternoon would develop into a full-scale céilidh disgorging onto the street, with many cheerful goodbyes, at nearer two in the morning. Perhaps because of its comparative isolation, even from Kinlochbuidhe all those 12 miles away, this fine tradition persisted in Lochuisge much longer than elsewhere – and to live there was truly like stepping back in time to the days of my parents or even my grandparents.

These informal gatherings at the post office or elsewhere and the implicit exchange of news, served not simply for idle gossip – although doubtless some titbits of another's misfortunes were much enjoyed. But this exchange of local news served as a strong cement helping to bind the community together; the farms and crofts which made up our community were scattered over a considerable area of many miles, such that we might not otherwise see some of our neighbours from one week to the next.

The regular exchange of, sometimes trivial, news during such 'drop-in' visits to other neighbours meant that wider community remained as tight-knit as an extended family – and let us know all the latest comings and goings even of those neighbours we had not seen for some time. Such meetings also served as an important mechanism for mobilising assistance if required. News might get out that someone had the flu, or perhaps had had a fall and could not get about, and as a response closer neighbours would call in for a chat, to take some fresh baking or to offer help – if only a lift to town to do the messages. But the grapevine served not only in case of accident or 'emergency'. No single-handed crofter ever had to ask for help with gathering sheep from hill grazings, or with the dipping, or clipping (shearing); simply everyone would know anyway what was planned and just turn up at the right time and place to offer extra hands. At least, always at the right place – even if time in the West Highlands is a more flexible commodity and the day's work might be delayed with another cup of tea and an exchange of gossip.

Besides these more impromptu gatherings, we had more structured entertainments. With an ageing population and no young children in the village, the village school attended by Dolly and Ina had long ago closed and – as in many other small communities – found a new lease of life as the Village Hall. Here were held animated whist drives (sufficiently animated to draw participants even the 12 miles from Kinlochbuidhe); every week the green baize was laid for carpet bowls – and every week during the winter, virtually the entire village turned out for an evening of Scottish country dancing.

Lochuisge's current postmistress, Seonaid, was a keen dancer, as was her immigrant husband Alastair and her sister, Kirsty – Ina's successor in delivering our post (or indeed any other commodity besides mail which one might require from the shop in Kinlochbuidhe, where the mailboat put in). Alastair was an enthusiastic devotee of Scottish country dance bands and traditional music, while both Seonaid and Kirsty were consummate dancers, the delicacy of their Highland schottische a joy to behold. Despite a natural reticence and lack of self-assurance, Kirsty was herself an inspiring instructor. Thus, once a week throughout the winter the fires would go on, Alastair would select a suitable range of fine tunes on tape, and Kirsty would coax us through the steps of a new set of jigs or reels to be learnt. Formal Scottish Country Dance (as promoted by the Royal Scottish Country Dance Society or RSCDS) is quite distinct from the so-called céilidh dances beloved of weddings and wakes, such as the Dashing White Sergeant, Canadian barn dances and Strip the Willow; these are more formal set dances: jigs and reels and stately strathspeys.

In fairness, abilities and experience were varied – from some who were regular dancers and probably competition class, to rank beginners. I myself had danced regularly, under my own mother's expert tutelage, until I was perhaps seven or eight years old, but never since. But all abilities were tolerated, there was no snobbery or 'side'; the more experienced dancers took it as their duty to guide the rest of us through each new dance until we were all at least proficient – and some of the novices even able to match or even outstrip those of the more experienced dancers who had throughout been cursed with no sense of rhythm or two left feet.

And the important thing about it was that we all had fun. We took it seriously, but for genuine pleasure rather than adopting some joyless, starchily disciplined approach affronted by any imperfection. Kirsty herself had a lively sense of the ridiculous, and her raucous cackle across the dance floor as we fell once more into disarray or missed some crucial change of tempo was unfailingly infectious. Perhaps (apart from the accompanying music) there was more than one reason we all especially enjoyed the intricate and very fast steps of Postie's Jig.

So, to the taped strains of Colin Dewar's Scottish Dance Band, of Bobby MacLeod from the neighbouring Mishnish Hotel on Mull, Fergie MacDonald, or my own favourite, Hector MacFadyen, we would take the floor and walk through the complex shapes and patterns of the Reel of the 51st[17] or some such. As always, for me it is the shapes of the finished dance which are so magical: the patterns that the dancers make on the floor with swirling skirts and kilts, and the close matching of the intricate steps to the repeated sets of the music. The White Heather Club[18] we were not, as time and again tall gentle Hamish the retired lorry driver, round-shouldered over his tiny but vivacious wife, Mairi, would lose the rhythm. The petite Mairi was an exceptional dancer, light on her feet, yet despite her years of training and constant light-hearted nagging, Hamish was always gangling and flatfooted as he stomped his way through an approximation to the steps, never attempting the proper heel and toe of the formal skipping step of the reel.

But we always got there more or less, with much merriment along the way. Alongside Alastair's recordings, our other mainstay was our own self-taught accordion player, young Niall the tractor driver, who surprised all, one New Year, closing the proceedings in front of a delighted Dolly and Hughina, by coaxing his piano accordion, or 'button box', into repeated, if somewhat strangled, 'coo-ees' in his own new composition: 'Ina's March to the Mill House'.

---

17 the 51st Highland Division
18 a 1960s BBC Scotland series showing off the best of traditional Scottish music and
    dancing

TOO MUCH CHOPPY

Dolly's cousin Donnie lived with his elderly mother Peigi in Kinlochbuidhe, but regularly scrounged a lift on a Friday evening to come and spend the weekend at Dolly's. He came really to play bowls in the Village Hall – held fortnightly throughout the autumn and winter – but always stayed on, making himself useful by chopping logs or kindling for the fire or working in the garden before his regular lift back to Kinlochbuidhe with the Minister after the end of the Sunday church service. Taking a lift with the Minister of course required him to sit through the service itself, which he endured with stoic calm and a pocket full of peppermints.

Donnie was severely handicapped: a motor cycle accident when he was 18 had resulted in serious head injuries and the insertion of several steel plates into his head to support the skull, and had left him with the arm and leg on one side virtually useless, as after a stroke; the accident had also robbed him of speech, and while he regained a remarkable ability to communicate, his speech was always laboured and slurred. Donnie was however not a quitter; he went to work initially for the sand quarry in Kinlochbuidhe: a labyrinthine network of tunnels stretching for miles under the village and the wider surrounding area like a gigantic Wookey Hole – a cavernous man-made cave system through which massive trucks (the same size as those more commonly seen above ground in the larger motorway developments) drove like Tonka toys. Sadly, while he was working in the mine, a detonator misfired and went off in his hand, wrenching three fingers from his good hand and blinding him permanently in one eye. Nothing daunted, he transferred his services to the Forestry until a machine harvester overturned on a slope above him, rolling down to trap and break both legs. On recovery he was transferred to lighter duties.

With his shambling gait and ill-formed speech many were fooled on first acquaintance into thinking Donnie perhaps retarded – the village half-wit. Far from it: despite his injuries Donnie had a shrewd intelligence and sharper eyesight with his one remaining eye than I could boast with two. And perhaps most remarkable of all, Donnie was never bitter about his accumulated misfortunes; he was a warm and generous man with a never-failing quirky sense of mischief.

Apart from the bowls, Donnie's passion was fishing, but clearly, given his disabilities, Peigi was concerned and distracted if he went out in his little boat alone; she always tried to persuade him to take company. In actual fact, once Donnie had rowed out in the little wooden dinghy to the open boat, once aboard and wedged in the stern, he was in his element and managed the little craft superbly well. Any disability became insignificant and irrelevant once seated with his arm draped over the tiller; he was an excellent and confident boatman, and perhaps out on the water, handling his boat with such skill, was the one place where Donnie could feel free and unhampered by his disability and on equal terms with any other able-bodied sailor. He also knew the waters very well and would guess unerringly where the mackerel would run.

I always knew when an invitation for a fishing trip was in the offing. The telephone would ring and my answering 'Hello' would be greeted by a long silence of concentration, punctuated by half-stammered beginnings as Donnie searched for the words. 'Busy?' he would enquire, or perhaps, 'Tomorrow? Busy?'

I enjoyed these outings so much that I quickly learnt to cancel any commitment I might have.

'Camas Inas; (a whispered) one, two, three, (a triumphant) *four* o'clock,' he would suggest (which meant I had to go and collect him and we would leave from Dolly's house) or 'Kinlochbuidhe, one, two, *three* o'clock'. If the arrangements were for the same day it was likely we would carry on; if however plans had been made for a day or two in advance, there was always the risk of the weather deteriorating and the disappointment of a subsequent phone call from Donnie – 'Too much choppy' – in cancellation of our trip.

The call would come and I would hot-foot it the 12 miles down the road to Kinlochbuidhe. Scrambling aboard the wee dinghy we would row out to Donnie's fishing boat. Despite his handicaps. Donnie was far from clumsy: he would often insist on rowing out himself. It was always Donnie who secured the dinghy rope to the mooring buoy. I would climb aboard first, but rarely needed to offer a helping hand as he scrambled from the dinghy. The outboard would be lowered and secured, and usually started first pull. (Indeed, only once were Peigi's fears realised, when the engine cut out in mid-channel, requiring a long row back to the mooring.) And then we would head off companionably to wherever Donnie had decided would be our fishing ground that day, while I assembled the rods and tied the feather lures and lead weights on our multi-hooked lines.

While I might spot a shoal of fish near the surface by the frenzied activities of a sudden aggregation of gulls, plunging into the water with tremendous fuss and commotion, Donnie always seemed to know where the deeper runs of larger fish would lie, yet with no obvious sign on the surface to guide him. Lining up the straight edge of a forestry plantation on one side, a spit jutting out from nearby Scarpay on another and with the ruined castle of Ardslignish to our bows, he would stop the engine and instruct us to lower our lines as the boat drifted slowly with wind and tide. After a few minutes, when he decided we had drifted too far off whatever invisible underwater feature he knew was channelling the mackerel, he would restart the engine, motor up the narrow fjord of the sea loch once more and we would start again our drift back with the current.

It was always peaceful out on the water, and Donnie was excellent company. Despite his problems with his speech, conversation was not difficult and he could always make understood what he was trying to say; doubtless I too, got more used to his way of speaking – and better at guessing in any case what he was likely to be saying. So between one thing and another we got along in comfortable companionship.

Until the mackerel struck. Suddenly the lines, which we were gently twitching up and down in the water to make twist and turn the feather lures attached to each of the multiple hooks, would go taut. Hasty exercise with the reel, and at the end a lifted rod: and a flashing, glittering mass of fish would sparkle in the sunlight. Our hooks were only lightly barbed and it was easy to shake the fish off, which were quickly dispatched and collected in a plastic barrel in the bottom of the boat. Lines were checked and cast again, because once one hits a run of mackerel, fishing is fast and furious.

Just as suddenly it is all over and cast lines dangle empty (another reason for keeping up the pressure when the fish *are* there). Mackerel are fierce predators of other smaller fish, even smaller mackerel, and are of course a food supply for bigger fish, so I felt no great guilt in our catch; and these clean fresh fish are indescribably beautiful with their barred backs and iridescent green and yellow patterning, the vivid colouring of fresh fish a far cry from the tired and muted colours of those on a fishmonger's slab. The excitement of the moment when they start to take the lures and the stunning beauty of the fish themselves made such outings a true delight for us.

Winding in our lines, we would motor back to Donnie's mooring buoy and row the dinghy back to shore, securing it behind the breakwater formed by the large wooden pier of the Calmac[19] ferry. Kinlochbuidhe made a pretty little harbour (and one of the most sheltered on that particular stretch of coast); many larger fishing villages around the coast – and particularly those doubling as ferry ports – have adopted Bobby MacLeod's highly successful idea for livening up a drab Tobermory harbour in the 1960s, and have painted the houses and shops around the waterfront in bright, primary colours which enhances their appeal, and not simply for the tourists. With the engine securely stowed and the oars hidden beneath the upturned dinghy, we carried the brimming barrel of fish back to my truck. And then to distribute the catch – for there was always far more there than we could use ourselves and mackerel do not freeze well – or at least do not keep long before they develop a rather rancid flavour.

---

19 Caledonian MacBrayne runs nearly all of the ferry services around Scotland's West Coast and islands.

Donnie would lever himself into the passenger seat and away we'd go to share the largesse. It was a great social excuse in its way, but perhaps also was a way in which Donnie could give something back to the community which loved and supported him. In truth everybody in Lethinnis knew Donnie, and I never met anyone who had not an enormous affection for him. His so-called disabilities counted for nothing in this place of extended family, and he was much loved for who he was – and for his irrepressible sense of humour.

First stop: his old friend Lindsay at the shop. Now Lindsay was an English incomer, having moved to Kinlochbuidhe many years before, but the shop was such a key focal point within the village (equal only to the church and the Social Club) and Lindsay was such a genuine and caring person, that she was fully accepted as part of the wider community. Indeed, in her role as postmistress and shopkeeper, dealing with the supply of tea and milk and the other necessities of a civilised life as well as paying out the regular pensions, she acted as watchdog and unpaid social worker for the village. For Lindsay, always the first to be aware if some regular customer had failed to come in for their newspaper or their weekly pension, would send her daughter Eilidh, or a neighbour, round with perhaps a box of teabags 'just to check everything was okay'. In this way the community operated its own support systems and in effect its own Social Services.

Delivery of the fish was one of the few occasions where one could escape after only the briefest of visits (sometimes less than an hour) and then it was off up the remote track to Saimhairidh to call on Mairead. Like almost everyone in Kinlochbuidhe – and like Dolly herself in Lochuisge – Mairead was related to Donnie, in this case yet another cousin. Her husband Iain worked on the fish farm, while, alongside running the croft, Mairead was the local seamstress, making and altering everything from clothes to curtains, and with her fine stitching, ensuring that much-loved garments lasted that little bit longer than they might otherwise have done, or could be stretched to encompass a growing embonpoint. My own kilt has so far expanded twice from its original design …

By comparison to 'remote' Lochuisge or neighbouring Camas Inas, relatively few in Kinlochbuidhe 'had the Gaelic' – certainly among those of Mairead's age, but she was a fluent Gaelic-speaker and both the family's daughters were brought up Gaelic-speaking. Indeed, while the Gaelic may largely have skipped Mairead's generation (when indeed, perhaps schoolteachers had discouraged use of the language and tried to encourage their pupils to speak the more cosmopolitan English, so that they did not appear such bumpkins), when I was there Gaelic was enjoying something of a resurgence among the younger folk. A surprising number of teenagers or those in their early 20s had at least a smattering of it. Yet this had nothing to do with an enforced learning of a declining language, as has perhaps happened in the past in Wales or in Ireland. Here, in very large part the recovery of interest in the Gaelic was due to a deeply ingrained culture of music and singing. Almost everybody played an instrument (with varying degrees of proficiency, it is true). Throughout the peninsula and on neighbouring Scarpay, almost everyone played the fiddle or the button box or the traditional Highland pipes. Many also sang (and sang very well), and it was perhaps a love for the old Gaelic airs and a need to understand better what they meant, in order to sing them with greater feeling and empathy, which explained why many of the younger people had at least some knowledge of Gaelic. Mairead's daughters, although not even in their teens, were no exception, and Rona, the elder, was an accomplished performer on the clarsach (or Gaelic harp) while younger sister Morven played an excruciating fiddle.

Moving on again, but now for relaxation and a glass of beer at the Social Club – handing the rest of the bucket of mackerel to Beathag behind the bar: a redoubtable woman who somehow managed to keep control within what was more generally a venue for serious drinkers, many of whom had to be forcibly ejected towards the end of the evening. There was little 'outside' entertainment in Kinlochbuidhe and as in many a west Highland town, the only real relaxation was the whisky – and it was a poor evening that did not end in a fight.

SUNDAY TEA

Despite our impatience, and in part because it had all been such a protracted business, when negotiations were over for the purchase of Allt na Mhuillin neither Morag nor I were in an immediate position to leave our jobs and move straight up to Lochuisge. Morag had to finish the school term while I myself owed it to my students at the University to see out the academic year. Yet we were uneasy about leaving the place unoccupied: not from any point of view of security, but simply because we did not want the Laird, after all his kindness, to think us unappreciative, or the village to draw the conclusion we were going to be absentee part-time holiday-makers. We wanted the house to be lived in and loved from the start. By great good fortune however, our close friend Ruth, who had been born and brought up near Edinburgh, also wanted to return more permanently to Scotland to live and – with no ties to the south, as we had – volunteered to move up at once keep the house warm for us, supervise initial repairs – and get to know the wider community. It was her declared intention to move on again once more when Morag and I were able to move into Allt na Mhuillin ourselves, although we knew the house was substantially bigger than our own needs, and we had every intention of asking Ruth to stay on after our own eventual removal.

So Ruth, along with Hamish, had been the advance guard – and indeed did stay on long after we ourselves had moved up there. Towing a large and old-fashioned caravan behind them (well, you never knew), they crawled the 600 miles north to Lochuisge. Hamish was Ruth's partner and boon companion – a three-legged mongrel bitch. Mis-sexed at birth (one wonders how?), Hamish was stuck with her birth name and there seemed little point in changing it – although it continued to confuse many.

She had lost one front leg in a traffic accident while a puppy, before Ruth had adopted her, but perhaps because it had happened so early had adapted surprisingly successfully, and although she had inevitably something of a dot-and-carry gait as she pegged along, she managed remarkably well. She also talked (or so Ruth's regular letters to us, before our own arrival in Lethinnis, gave us to understand); indeed Hamish would even, on occasion, dictate letters to us herself, or messages to Holly and Bandit, our own dogs of the time:

Dear Bandit,

I DON'T like that car because my bed isn't comfy in it – and when I complain, SHE puts my blanket on the seat instead and I don't like that EITHER, 'cos it doesn't feel very SAFE. I don't understand why we have to spend so much time in it, rather than just staying at home. I have to say I am not a seafaring dog either. I don't LIKE it when she keeps getting on those nasty bouncy things – it's all very NASTY and she should comfort me with chocolate biscuits now and again. But the smells are nice here and the deer are nice because they don't seem to mind me. Anyway, I am confused because SHE keeps telling me that you are going to be coming soon, all of you, and I keep rushing to the door and looking out and waiting and waiting, but you don't come. So ARE you coming and if so why aren't you HERE yet?

or

Dear Bandit,

I'm sorry you have got nothing for your birthday. I did

remember and nagged her to get something to send from that nice shop in Kilmory. Well, that shop was closed, but she did get something else (which looked pretty naff actually – although it was edible, come to think of it). But she had it all ready to go and then went and left it on her desk and when we went to get it a whole lot of little bits of paper showered down and SOMEONE small and nosey had been having a nibble!

I am VERY cross – I would rather have eaten it myself – but she wouldn't even let me have the rest of it and threw it OUT; can you BELIEVE it? She said it might be germy or something (what is that?). So now I have nothing to send. She always TELLS me that the shop just down the road is not the right sort of shop for that sort of thing (but she never actually lets me go in to look).

So please forgive me. You'll just have to have ANOTHER birthday when you get here …

Hamish was also called upon to act as intermediary in case of possible disasters:

Hello again. She says I've got to tell you because she's too scared. But when we got home from Scarpay yesterday we found lots of water running down the wall of our bedroom. SHE said something I didn't understand (it sounded foreign) and ran away in the car which I thought was a pretty useless thing to do. Anyway, she did come back with some ladders and did some peculiar acrobatics on the roof. She had to go to the second top rung on the ladder and lean out a long way which I found pretty frightening because she hadn't given me my dinner and I was worried that if she fell off I'd be awfully hungry for a very long time until someone happened past the next day. Anyway she didn't, but she was up there for AGES and I was getting VERY hungry and fed up and then she started throwing things down and I was frightened so I ran

*inside. Then, just when I thought I MIGHT get some dinner,
she disappeared INSIDE through the little hole in the ceiling.*

*I don't know what she was doing, but she talked some more
foreign stuff and when she came down she was covered in
cobwebs ... But she says it's all right now.*

In this way and through Ruth's own regular letters, we did keep in
contact with the community we were about to embrace. Ruth herself
organised urgent and immediate repairs (those which would not wait
until our arrival) and sent us scurrilous but informative pen pictures
of those who were to become our new neighbours to such effect that
we felt we knew many of them as old friends by the time we ourselves
arrived. She also sent us cameos of what to expect: the otters loafing
amongst the bladder wrack of the strandline, the roe deer timidly
grazing in our two future goat fields and the first time they dared to
bring with them tiny spotted kids, the glory of the spring flowers –
and how, with such a short summer season in the north, everything
seemed to burst into flower at once.

And she proved an excellent ambassador for our own later arrival.
Ruth was a tall, gentle redhead, with a tangled mane of chestnut hair,
a self-effacing soul who never pushed herself forward, who always
saw the other point of view – and she quickly became a much-loved
member of the village, drawn in to manage the produce stall at the
village fair, to help with the teas and coffees for the whist, to play the
keyboard for church (quickly substituting a selection of haunting
Gaelic airs for the normally-expected but dreary religious pieces
required for the introit and exeunt before and after the service itself).
She and Hamish became firm friends and firm favourites with Dolly –
and were accorded the ultimate accolade. It is said that eavesdroppers
never hear good of themselves, but Ruth was quietly delighted when
she heard Dolly confide to her lifelong friend Ina, 'She's one of us, Ina;
she's not like Cindy.[20] Not that Cindy wasn't nice enough, but she was
never one of *us*, and Ruth is; she's the same as us.'

---

20 a previous tenant of Allt na Mhuillin, some years earlier

And Dolly herself was loyal to a fault. It was Dolly who had shown me over Allt na Mhuillin when I had viewed all those months before; Dolly who had insisted I stop for a cup of tea and some home-made scones in her Mill House after I had looked over Allt na Mhuillin; Dolly, I am convinced, who put in a good word for me with the Laird after my visit and persuaded him to sell to us.[21]

After we had ourselves joined Ruth at Allt na Mhuillin and taken over at least some part of the house for our own use, Sunday afternoon tea with Dolly quickly became an established tradition. As Ruth delivered her home after the church service, we would follow down the road and join them at the Mill House. In fact afternoon tea was perhaps something of a euphemism, for it took some weeks to persuade the ever-hospitable Dolly that a large whisky at 3 o'clock of a summer's afternoon was not an essential part of her duties as hostess and we would not consider her failing in her duties if we actually *did* content ourselves with a cup of tea.

In winter it was my given task to light the coal stove while Dolly busied herself with the electric kettle and tea-making, and buttered the scones or pancakes prepared earlier for our tea. If Donnie was up for the weekend he would settle himself into his accustomed chair in the corner and they would start to talk and reminisce; on these occasions I always regretted not taking some discreet tape-recorder to capture for ever their stories of the local history (and most significantly, who was related to whom; who had become divorced from whom, and who had later remarried whom in the intricate network of village politics: all crucial information if one was not to put a foot wrong in the delicate sensitivities of a small and intricate community). Some of the stories she would tell were indeed hilarious (even without the Scotch), and always punctuated by Dolly's screaming cackle of laughter and Donnie's quieter rumbling chuckle.

Apart from her brief period in service in far-distant Clydebank, Dolly had lived at the Mill House all her life. She was a small bird-

---

21 Under the Scottish system of sale, a house may be sold not necessarily to the highest bidder, but to the person who the seller thinks most suited, who he or she thinks will best fit into the community. This is actually an extremely important consideration in remote rural areas where everyone must strive to get on with each other – and makes the experience of house purchase not dissimilar to a job interview!

like creature with thick pebble glasses: as round and apple-cheeked as her friend Ina was tall and gaunt, although it quickly became apparent that at least some of the round rosiness was due to the heavy doses of steroids she consumed on a regular basis to keep her persistent asthma and erratic heart under control. This ill-health did mean that she herself rarely visited; it had clearly been a struggle for her to walk as far as Allt na Mhuillin to show me around, and shortly after we had arrived she stopped her regular daily walk up to the kitchen in the Big House, instead accepting a lift each day from the handyman, John Angus. But she continued that daily pilgrimage until she died: service in the Big House was her job (even if, truth be told, she sat in the kitchen most of the day dozing in front of the giant Aga and the Laird paid her modest wages in return for very little practical assistance; but she had offered the better part of a lifetime's service to The Aunt).

Ruth became, unobtrusively – and, to an extent unwillingly – her carer and social worker, for Dolly became increasingly unable to get about, and relied for company on people calling on her. Ruth herself, like me, was self-employed. She had been born and brought up as the daughter of the Manse in Colinton outside Edinburgh, and in the course of a varied career had worked as a book-keeper and accountant, run a pub, then run a garage until she had ended up going to university as a mature student. Having become increasingly involved in what we might call environmental issues, she was intelligent enough to be concerned that she was being asked to sign up to opinions and crusades on behalf of Friends of the Planet or Green Earth or whatever organisation it might be, when she did not necessarily have the complete facts, but only what (potentially biased) interpretation of events she might have been fed by these activist organisations. So she determined to inform herself more fully and enrolled in a degree course in Environmental Sciences. I greatly admired this attitude and commitment (which I later met in a surprising number of my own mature students returning to study as adults). After completing her degree, however, she was determined to return to Scotland, and so reverted to her former profession as accountant and book-keeper.

She hated it (and was always in the most terrible muddle with her own finances if meticulous in the affairs of others.) but it was a

45

living – and made bearable in that for the most part she was working for small local businesses all over the peninsula: local shops, fencing contractors, crofters, small farmers, those running bed & breakfast businesses. This offered an introduction to lots of local people she might otherwise never have encountered and, where she was able to help resolve financial difficulties or offer advice to get the business on a better commercial footing, was a way in which she could feel she was already giving something back to the community in return from the pleasure she derived from being a part of it. And the tales she *could* share of her clients, without a breach of confidence: I remember her recounting, with tears in her eyes, the predicament of one old crofter from Mull who, like the rest of us never locked his door or indeed took the key from his car – after all you never know when a neighbour might need to borrow a vehicle in an emergency if their own was for some reason broken down. Having taken the ferry across to Oban for a rare shopping expedition, the bodach decided that perhaps in this comparative metropolis full of strangers, he should perhaps lock his car when he left it in the car park – only to discover, to his certain chagrin, that in the damp and salty atmosphere of coastal Mull, the key had become rusted immovably in the ignition! He had to take his chances and trust that people in Oban were as honourable as those of his native Mull (they are, whatever the Duke of Edinburgh's list of ten good things about Oban, including the fact that it was an easy place to get out of) but the whole episode said so much about the trusting nature of island life.

THE WEEKLY VAN

The post office at Camas Inas was a remarkable structure, largely reminiscent of a small garden shed, although both roof and walls were sheathed in brightly-painted corrugated iron (in the manner of those old-fashioned dwellings which were originally called 'bungalows'). There were two doors: one through which Seonaid could access the minuscule space behind the wooden counter, and one in front for customers. This larger area could nonetheless accommodate at most two persons and was in any event usually already occupied by Alastair's large and ragged sheepdogs (taking advantage of what little shelter there was for them in the farmyard). In truth Seonaid was rarely in residence anyway, and it was much simpler just to go and chap the back door of the croft-house. The downside of this arrangement (at least surely from Seonaid's point of view) was the inevitable cup of coffee and céilidh which would result, even if in the end, as you perhaps took your leave, she did accompany you across to the green shed to dispense a stamp or a postal order or whatever might have been the primary purpose of the visit.

Even that might take some time. Seonaid was *not* au fait with the latest rules and regulations the Post Office in its wisdom might have come up with – nor did she really seem to know on which of the various shelves ingeniously installed by Alastair in the tiny space behind the counter might lurk the appropriate form or piece of paper you had come to request. This, together with the unbroken continuation of whatever conversation had begun in her living room, meant that some considerable time might be taken processing even the simplest request. But as in Kinlochbuidhe, the post office – and Seonaid's croft-house – was in some ways the social hub of the little village and the hub from which intelligence and assistance flowed to all our closer and more distant neighbours among the scattered community of isolated crofts and farmsteads it served.

It was also the staging post for the weekly visit of the mobile grocery van. This could very well disrupt detailed negotiations over a request for a motor vehicle taxation form in the tiny post office – and was probably the only event likely to interrupt a gathering of neighbours in the ever-hospitable croft-house kitchen. Andy-the-Van's arrival was greeted by everyone with the greatest of pleasure, and all piled out to buy the weekly shop as well as catch up on news from further-flung villages Andy had visited on his rounds. In truth, in these days of supermarkets and domestic freezers, many of the villagers did their main shopping in the county town back across the ferry. For older residents who did not drive, those of us who were going 'into town' would take a shopping list and buy on their behalf, but that is never quite the same thing – and the weekly arrival of the van allowed them to still maintain a modicum of independence and most importantly, not only do their own 'messages' but choose little luxuries for themselves. Even those of us who did shop in town would allow ourselves a weekly treat.

Andy-the-Van sold everything from somewhat tired vegetables to almost anything which could be purchased in a tin, to Tunnock's tea cakes, to somewhat garishly iced fancies and sweets for the children – in those villages which had children. Despite the lack of children in Lochuisge he still did a surprisingly good trade, since many of the adults had a sweet tooth or two and enjoyed the jelly snakes or the pink sugar shrimps as much as any child. And it was in any case a pleasantly social occasion – as long as it wasn't raining too hard and the midges were at peace. He would park up the van, open the two rear doors and take down from in front of the counter a wooden block or 'pop-up' of two steps to enable those less sound in wind and limb to climb up into the van itself. Then the leisurely business of trade would commence, while those waiting in their turn (it was hardly a queue) gossiped happily or indulged in anticipatory decision-making as to which of the delights on offer this week they might actually purchase. Despite the fact that he had indubitably already had a very long day and would doubtless visit other villages before returning home, it was never rushed, and Andy never seemed hurried or impatient.

Indeed, if we happened not to be at the post office in time for his arrival, he would never-failingly drive on to Allt na Mhuillin itself after closing the doors at Camas Inas, just to see if there was anything we might need. I genuinely have no idea how he made a living.

Although Andy-the-Van can hardly have had another job, since his days on the road were long enough, it is true that most of the villagers had more than one job to make ends meet, and to meet ends: to supply the various services people needed supplied. Many of those, even with full-time jobs on the Estate, or in the forestry or the fish farm, nonetheless had crofts or smallholdings, and managed their sheep and cattle in evenings or weekends, with a day off to go to the local market with their stock when the sales were on. If you wanted your car serviced at the garage, you had to be sure that Iain the mechanic was not away at his second job as a stalker/ghillie on one of the local Estates, while Lindsay in the Kinlochbuidhe shop doubled as senior officer in the local fire brigade. Even in town, no one seemed to have just a single job or supply a single commodity. It took me years to learn that if you wanted a sheet of glass you have to go to the undertaker; while Gillies' the Ironmonger and purveyor of household goods in Kilmory also boasted the finest range of malt whiskies for miles around.

EARNING A LIVING

I myself had outside work. Unlike the majority of the locals, our crofting was in no sense commercial and was more a case of needing to work the land appropriately to keep it in good order and to provide some level of self-sufficiency in meat, eggs, milk and dairy products and vegetables. We did in fact produce all our own milk, butter and some soft cheeses and – at least until the arrival of the peafowl – grew more than enough vegetables for our own use. Each year we put lambs and surplus cockerels and a venison carcass in the freezer – but like others we also needed a cash income to pay for other essentials such as fuel, toilet rolls and electricity.

I thus travelled on and off the peninsula and across the ferry at the Narrows with fair frequency, but I never found the journey tiresome or tiring. In times of hurry I could do the journey in a little over an hour, but in truth I rarely hurried. There were always things to watch along the road and at the narrow pass at the top of the ridge. Often I would see red deer grazing alongside the road or stop to watch eagles or buzzards soaring in the thermals along the rock buttresses of the summit ridge.

Equally often the road would be blocked by a flock of sheep or group of cattle meandering along a path of least resistance from one favoured grazing area to another, or perhaps being moved more forcibly by one of the local shepherds. This too was time to stop and wind down the window and catch up with the 'craic'.

The single-track roads were quiet, but every so often I would meet an oncoming vehicle, and one or other would have to reverse to a passing place cut into the verge at intervals to allow for passage – or for overtaking, if some vehicle appearing in the rear-view mirror was in some foolish rush. I quickly memorised a visual map of all passing places along the route so knew intuitively which was the nearest and thus if meeting an approaching vehicle, which of the two should probably engage reverse. But in truth, most of the vehicles I met were those of other locals and when drawn alongside in the chosen passing point, the windows wound down once more until conversation was interrupted by the next approaching vehicle needing to pass. In this way it never seemed a long journey to the Narrows, and indeed the road was a familiar one and I knew the owners of all the crofts and farms along the route, so that the journey always felt more like a voyage among friends – and an opportunity to spy on the latest changes and innovations I might note in my more distant neighbour's fields and farmsteads. ('Did you see that Lachie's put up a new tractor shed?' 'I see that Ewen's started the clipping early.')

The only time the journey palled was if I was truly in a hurry, or if the ferry was off – which necessitated an additional hour and a half's drive around the head of the loch, through less familiar territory. This unexpected addition could be a serious blow, especially on return journeys when I might already have driven for a good many hours only to discover there was an unexpected three more to go instead of the anticipated hour or so. But in large part the ferry was predictable and only off in the very worst of weathers, on Christmas Day and Boxing Day, and for two days over the New Year. And although over the summer it provided for an extensive tourist traffic, it, like the road to Kinlochbuidhe and Lochuisge beyond, was a great meeting point for locals and yet another chance for a gossip with neighbours or the ferry crew. We loved the ferry, which provided a pleasant social break on journeys out, and a welcome reassurance of a return to a gentler pace of life on journeys home: time to take a deeper breath and relax into that slower, more familiar rhythm of Lethinnis. The brief crossing indeed marked a gateway between two worlds.

I continued to work as a wildlife biologist but had now chosen to put my money more where my mouth had been. Instead of lecturing and doing research on the biology of our native wildlife and their impact on their environment, I had decided the time had come to put that accumulated knowledge into practice, using that increased understanding of the animals and their ecology to develop new and perhaps more subtle ways of managing their more damaging impacts. In a sense I had set up shop as a troubleshooter, called out to advise on management of deer and other larger wildlife species when problems arose – perhaps damage to agricultural or forestry interests, perhaps where impacts were proving excessive of fragile natural habitats, or simply to resolve conflicts of interest between neighbours, or ensure that ongoing management might be more sustainable from both an economic and ecological standpoint. Apart from the millions of free-roaming sheep, deer are probably the most significant ecological factors shaping the dynamics of ecological systems throughout the Highlands, so for the most part this work resolved to the development of innovative solutions to problems caused by red and sika deer.

The problems were usually simple – if finding the solution which would satisfy everyone was not.

Thus one landowner might wish to maintain high densities of deer on the open moorland in order to support the economics of an Estate which was based largely around deer-stalking and the production of venison, while his immediate neighbour wanted to grow trees without necessarily suffering the expense of extensive fencing. Or that neighbour might be more interested in the sporting income to be made from grouse than in deer, and had perhaps concerns that high densities of deer in the wider landscape might be contributing to increased levels of tick and tick-borne diseases which might affect the productivity of grouse broods. Or perhaps the densities of deer aspired to in order to sustain a historic level of harvest and revenue might now be considered by Scottish Natural Heritage, our statutory conservation agency, to be causing excessive damage on designated Sites of Special Scientific Interest (or SSSIs). My role in a nutshell was to see if there might be some middle course where all could have their cake and eat it. Those close to the problem often find it difficult to step back and look for alternative solutions because 'it has always been done like this'; in many cases in addition, a long history of ongoing conflict had led to entrenched and polarised positions between the warring neighbours. My job was thus (and remains) as practical peacemaker in exploring the potential for delivering each landowner's sporting or other income in a slightly different way which will reduce conflict and at the same time may provide a more sustainable and more environmentally sensitive management overall. In practice this translates to being allowed to walk out in some of the most remote places, amongst some of the most beautiful scenery in Scotland, alone but for the deer and the eagles and perhaps the company of the Estate's own experienced stalker – and get paid for it.

It is hard to convey the grandeur of that backdrop. As I sit writing this, I look at from my desk to the imposing bulk of Ben Nevis, the fissured buttresses of the North Face, Coire Leis, the rocky arête north-west to Carn Mor Dearg and Aonach Mor, and beyond to the many peaks of the Nevis range of hills. There is snow on the tops, even in June. High plateaux of scree and wind-clipped heath are interspersed in the depressions of deeper peat with the nodding cotton-grass of blanket bog and innumerable small pools and 'dubh-lochs' of bogbean. It is a wide landscape haunted by the echoing calls of curlew and red-throated diver. Over on the East Coast – in, say, Sutherland or Caithness – there are big skies across the Moray Firth; each coastal village has its own small harbour in some sheltered inlet giving an unexpected flash of colour from the clustered fishing boats, amongst the more muted tones of the rocky cliffs. In the far north, wide empty beaches of silver sand buffeted by the crashing waves of the Pentland Firth.

And in the autumn the whole changes; as the bracken turns to astonishing shades of russet, the ubiquitous deer-grass turns a glorious orange, the hills take on a tapestry weave of colours that no one would ever believe who has not visited the Highlands of Scotland. I have hanging in my office a screenprint by Ishbel Macdonald of whooper swans coming in to land on the still waters of an inland loch. The swans themselves are caught in a glow of light and the hills behind are a riot of orange and red and purple that make the whole seem almost like an abstraction. But in truth this is no fantasy or artist's 'translation' of the scene to something more reminiscent of Jolomo's palette, but honestly reflects the colours which dress these hillsides at this time of year. If, that is, you can see them at all for the rain and the low cloud.

Today, I was on my way to Glenaladale. This lovely Estate stretches some 7 miles along the north-west shore of Loch Shiel from Glenfinnan and the monument erected by Alexander Macdonald, 10th Laird of Glenaladale, to commemorate the raising of the Jacobite standard in 1745. There are no roads within the Estate and one must perforce walk its length or access it by boat along the loch. At its southern –or western – limit, Glenaladale borders with Gaskan in the Camas Grianach, for a time home to the naturalist and writer Mike Tomkies. Glenaladale's problem was comparatively simple – at least in principle – in that the Estate relies on stalking as a source of income and to ensure sufficient revenue to justify continued employment of the Estate stalker; yet at the same time it was clear that browsing by red deer was inhibiting regeneration of the historic Atlantic oakwoods which fringe the shore of the loch, such that no young saplings were surviving to grow to maturity and replace the more mature trees in their turn as these became senescent. In fact the background was illuminating. A thriving coastal woodland persists towards Gaskan on the western side of the Glenaladale River – with trees of mixed ages testifying to a continuing regeneration within the woodland. Yet to the east of the river, little or no regeneration had survived and the woodland was already fragmented and largely moribund.

The irony of the situation was that deer densities were much lower in this area than at Gaskan. In the distant past, however, sheep had been run on this part of the Estate to the east of the river, but never across the river at Gaskan. It was apparent that current densities of deer were not such as to cause damage to a vigorous and healthy woodland, but once the initial damage had been done (in this case by sheep) even comparatively low densities of deer were sufficient to inhibit recovery – yet the Estate could not afford to reduce densities much lower without sacrificing the income from the stalking and then the stalker himself.

There was only a scattering of snow on the shore line as we picked our way down from the lodge and past the remains of the many charcoal-burners' kilns – sobering evidence that the woodland had indeed been much more productive in times past; but as we headed out from the shelter of the fringe of trees which still skirt the lochside, a crisp covering deepened underfoot. Groups of hinds and calves stood and watched us pass from the bottom of some of the deeper corries. While red deer have become remarkably well adapted to the open moorland which covers much of the Scottish uplands, cold and wind-chill are the real enemy, draining energy and stripping condition faster than the meagre pickings of winter food supplies can replace it. Cold itself is rarely an issue, but the effects of wind-chill on a wet coat can translate the ambient temperature to the equivalent of ten degrees lower, and so the deer seek shelter from anything but the lightest breeze. We climbed on: the best way to get a feel for how a landscape hangs together (and how in turn the deer might use its varied resources) is to get to a central high point for an all-round perspective. The deer stayed in the lower corries, but as we climbed, ptarmigan cackled their way out of range among the more exposed rocky cairns, visible only because of the black eye markings and black tip to the tail of their all-white winter coat.

At the top of Beinn Mhic Cedidh we paused for the panorama, flinching involuntarily as the scream of jet engines heralded the passing of some fighter jet on exercise – too frequent a scourge of the shattered peace of the Highlands, where the 'empty' countryside is considered a fair training-ground for high-speed jets. I scanned the skies around but couldn't see the plane until Davie caught my arm and pointed downwards, where the sunlight glinted on the back of the aeroplane banking away far below us. Somehow I can never get accustomed to the idea of looking down to spot aircraft.

THE RED DEER 'PROBLEM'

I myself am no stalker – at least, one only armed with a camera – although I accept that in the absence of natural predators deer populations need to be managed to control their numbers and their impacts on the vegetation, and if some paying 'guest' can be persuaded to give the Estate money for the dubious privilege of being the one to pull the trigger, so be it. It is a significant source of income for landholdings on marginal land with very few alternative forms of land-use, and it provides much-needed employment in these fragile rural communities. The majority of full-time stalkers or ghillies, like all gamekeepers, are keen naturalists and good observers – and indeed, for most of the guests, the real pleasure of the stalk has less to do with the final kill than the opportunity to spend a day on the hill with these knowledgeable and informative guides and in admiring their fieldcraft in eventually getting the client close to a 'shootable' stag. Many guests return year after year to the same Estate, in large part because of the bond they have formed with these experienced hill-men.

On a dry day at least, and high enough on the hill to be clear of the inevitable midges, there is something extraordinarily uplifting in picking your way carefully across a rocky hillside, ankle-deep in purple heather, or skirting around peat hags full of sphagnum moss and gently waving cotton-grass and with distant views of high peaks across the other side of some basin corrie.

Apart from the low-flying fighter jets out on manoeuvres, there is an uninterrupted sense of peace and timelessness – and there is always something to see: dragonflies disporting themselves above the many shallow bog pools, red-throated divers on the larger lochans, the cries of curlew or the occasional grouse, and the spectacular summit heaths of dwarf, wind-clipped heather interspersed with colourful lichens, reindeer moss and clubmoss.

Management of red deer herds and their impacts has however become, in recent years a very contentious issue – and much bound up with political views in some quarters against private ownership of Scotland's land, and the whole concept of wealthy landowners (or wealthy clients) with time on their hands 'amusing' themselves in shooting deer (or it might be grouse) as a recreational pursuit. All debate is tinged with this undercurrent of alternative agenda.

No one would dispute that populations of red deer have increased tremendously in number over recent years. Figures published by the Deer Commission for Scotland suggest that red deer numbers in the Highlands of Scotland have doubled over the last 30 years and are now in excess of 300,000. Increasing incidence of damage to agriculture and forestry is reported; conservation bodies point to the deterioration of heather uplands due to overgrazing and the lack of regeneration in native woodland; newspapers and magazines carry horrific photographic montages telling of huge numbers of deer starving to death each winter or succumbing to exposure because of their poor condition.

It is widely argued that there are simply too many deer in the Highlands, and a number of conservation agencies are now calling for statutory controls on red deer density: with the Deer Commission already empowered to require landowners to reduce deer numbers on their land where appropriate (specifically, where there is perceived to be serious damage to agricultural, forestry or conservation interests, or where it is considered that rising numbers pose an increased threat of road traffic accidents). Whether country dweller or city office worker, young or old, surely every Scot is aware of the debate, and it is an issue on which opinions are strongly divided and strongly held. Yet often those opposing viewpoints are each based upon incomplete information or misinformation; while the very fact of its high profile and extensive media publicity has enabled many a taproom politician to adopt a firm stand on the matter, ironically much of that same media coverage has been sensational, emotive and itself unbalanced.

To begin with, the actual total number of wild red deer in Scotland (or indeed the overall numbers of any other deer species) is not a particularly helpful figure anyway. Red deer densities vary tremendously in different parts of the country: the Deer Commission's own figures suggest densities typically between 4 and 10 deer per square kilometre for much of the (mainland) area counted; only in one or two areas are really high densities recorded – perhaps as high as 30 or 40 deer per square kilometre. In practice therefore, over much of the country deer densities are comparative low (and relatively stable). While clearly the precise threshold depends to an extent on climate and productivity of the soil, a rule of thumb suggests that woodland regeneration can occur in the absence of any fences at densities of deer of the order of 3 or 4 per square kilometre, while densities of deer at between 7 and 8 deer per 100 hectares are generally considered ideal for maintaining heathland and other open hill habitats in good condition.

It is only in certain particular areas that populations have built up numbers to relatively high densities – and more especially, instead of being scattered across the landscape in small parcels of half a dozen to a dozen, animals have coalesced into large and very mobile herds which 'pour over the hillside like brown gravy'. In some of these areas, where deer do occur at high density, they may have a significant impact. But even then, this is not necessarily a problem. Impact, however high, only translates to 'damage' if the impact recorded conflicts with (completely human-based) judgements for what is appropriate, and where recorded impacts conflict in some way with primary land-use objectives. Damage is thus in the eye of the beholder, when impact is assessed against actual management objectives. Nor should we presume that those unacceptable impacts occur generally. Despite, again, the media hype, negative impacts are not universal, but tend to be very local in their effect.

Perhaps, to the general public perhaps the most powerful case for intervention is made by the increasing number of reported cases of mass overwinter mortality. Newsprint photographs of piles of carcasses shock the sensibilities; stories at the breakfast table of Estates using JCBs to dig holes big enough to bury their dead, and others with 'lorry-loads' of corpses are unpalatable to say the least. It is argued that such die-offs must be reflect a massive overstocking of the range, and that on simple welfare grounds we have a moral responsibility to reduce numbers so that they are once more within the capacity of the range to support them. But this argument, too, is complex: recent increases in deer numbers may at least in part be due to an actual increase in the number the ground can support due to a reduction in competition from sheep. Further, there is little evidence to suggest that high overwinter mortality is related in any simple way to density. It would appear that most of such episodes of heavy mortality are more closely related to weather conditions than to density. While animals on restricted grazing and therefore in poor condition may be less able to withstand extremes of winter weather, many of the deer which have died in the most recent episodes of heavy mortality were apparently in relatively good condition – even animals receiving supplementary food succumbed. Major mortality events are correlated more closely with prolonged rain on the West Coast or extended spells of sub-zero temperature in the Central and Eastern Highlands than they are to population density – and certainly such mortality should not be blamed on failure of managers to exert an adequate control on numbers.

A wide variety of factors is likely to affect the number of deer a piece of ground can support, including topography and shelter offered, nature of the vegetation and its quality as forage, history of grazing and burning – and climate. An equal variety of factors may influence the degree of damage inflicted by a population of deer of a given size on agriculture, forestry or natural vegetational communities of conservational value; thus levels of damage will be influenced again by topography, soil type, climate, availability of alternative foodstuffs etc. Nor is it yet sufficiently well-established what may be the relative importance of deer as opposed to sheep grazing in the decline of upland vegetation or inhibition of regeneration in woodland – and there is clearly also a direct interaction between the two in that deer densities are themselves not independent of changing sheep numbers in the uplands. Finally, even those catastrophic winter die-offs that so catch the public eye are apparently not related in any simple way to deer population density alone, and at present we have no real data on the extent to which even enhanced levels of culling can reduce that mortality.

It would seem that much of the ongoing debate is motivated by more a more political agenda about landownership and recreational stalking. What in effect is important about all of this, however, is the fact that it is clear that red deer in Scotland are what ecologists refer to as a keystone species: that is, they have a significant, and shaping, effect within the ecosystems in which they occur.

In effect they are one of the most significant engineers of habitat change. Thus – and this is perhaps the most important bit: management of deer cannot be separated from more general management of wild land. Their effects on their habitat are so pronounced that in effect management of deer populations cannot be divorced from wider management of the entire landscape of which they are perhaps, along with the ubiquitous hill sheep, the single most significant shaping influence.

THE VILLAGE HALL

The village school at Camas Inas, where Dolly and Ina had laboured over their desks as children, had closed long ago, but the single schoolroom had been rented back to the community for a peppercorn rent for use as a village hall. Indeed, as I write, it has now been sold to the village for the princely sum of £1. Like other buildings in Cama Inas it was solidly built of stone and slate; even in its working days it had been a single room with a small lean-to kitchen attached to one corner. It was actually a tall space, dominated by an enormous window at one end of almost church-like proportions; while not of stained glass the glazing panels were nonetheless supported by stone mullions – and in the West Coast weather it leaked incessantly. The same dampness penetrated the plaster walls above the dado rail which topped the cladding of plank panelling extending over the lower half of each wall. Perhaps it was no wonder that in the end the council decided to relinquish all responsibility for its upkeep. In an attempt to brighten it up and perhaps ensure its transition in the memories of the older folk from one-time schoolroom to community hall, the plaster of the upper half of the walls had been painted a bright mustard yellow, while the panelling below the dado rail was of an extraordinarily bilious lime green.

Under the end window was an old-fashioned glass-fronted bookcase which housed the small library of books, of which perhaps a third were exchanged every two weeks with the fortnightly arrival of the mobile library. This unprepossessing space was in turns library and polling station for elections, but also the venue over the winter for the weekly evening of bowls, the country dancing and less regular but hilarious (and fiercely competitive) evenings of table-tennis; if Hamish the Lorry was perhaps not the most elegant of dancers with seemingly no long-term or even short-term memory for the steps, he was a demon table-tennis player. Two or three nights in the week over the winter, there would be something on in the Hall, and we all made a point of attending as much as we could (although I confess I was not a regular attender at the whist drives). Such regular events tended to stop over the summer, with the advent of longer daylight and lighter evenings, because most of the villagers had work to do on the croft while daylight lasted; but they were a godsend during the longer evenings of the darker winter months.

And twice a year, Lochuisge and Camas Inas would hold a more formal céilidh in the Hall. These more organised entertainments in the Village Hall were totally different from the informal gatherings which took place in people's houses, and grew like a crystal as more and more people dropped by and brought their instruments. The Village Hall céilidhs were far more structured and, while enjoyed by all, were a bit more stilted – at least in the early part of the evening – with everyone sitting in the old school chairs ranged around the outside walls of the hall and each in turn invited up to perform their chosen party-piece by the Master of Ceremonies for the evening, or 'Fear an Tighe'. Such an event would be scheduled for 7 o'clock or even 8 in the evening – well after dark, so that all might have finished their evening chores on the croft. Gradually the hall would fill, because everybody turned up to such occasions, but it might well be half-past eight or nine before handsome young Johnny Soutar, Fear an Tighe for the night, called for our attention in order to make a start. Act after act would stand and perform – all of them of course well known to Johnny, who introduced each with some wisecrack or another, to general mirth and hilarity.

The emphasis in the early evening was on any children present, who would perhaps be leaving before the night was finished, to be hustled home to bed. While Lochuisge had no children itself, some of the more scattered crofts or farms had families, and all children were brought up from infancy with music around them and always encouraged to perform. Rona Campbell would play a delicate air on the clarsach, and her six-year-old sister Morven would follow with a somewhat laboured piece on the fiddle – but all were applauded equally for their efforts, and it was an excellent way to encourage them and encourage their continued love of music – and performing.

Johnny would remind us of the tale told of the village postmistress in neighbouring Kilchoan who had, on some occasion, shut the post office with no warning. One of the local pensioners, who had been to collect her weekly pension, had remonstrated with her about the lack of warning, and the following day there appeared a notice on the post office door 'Closed Today (and closed yesterday, too)' – an apocryphal tale, told I am sure of every village post office, but fresh to me that evening.

Then the older folk would get their turn, with a recitation of some Gaelic poem passed down through the generations by word of mouth – perhaps a section of Duncan Ban McIntyre's 'Ode to Beinn Dobhrain' – or just as likely a rendition of 'Albert an t-Lion'. As well as these more impromptu acts there were also some scheduled pieces, perhaps by Alma's daughter Catriona, who lived away now but had recently (and repeatedly) won the National Mod (the national festival devoted to Gaelic culture) as a singer of the old Gaelic songs. Catriona had a full and haunting voice; these traditional songs – whether laments for a lover drowned at the fishing never to return, or waulking songs (created to keep the rhythm for the woman pummelling and kneading the soaked fleeces to soften them in readiness for weaving) – these songs were always sung unaccompanied, and many is the time the beauty of Catriona's pure melodies would reduce me to involuntary tears.

As the evening wore on, the rear door to the hall would quietly open and close as some of the men slipped outside into the fresh air. As the atmosphere inside the hall grew a little fuggy, these disappearances would grow to a steady trickle. But after an interval each would return and resume his seat.

I was reminded of the amusing statistic reported to me by one of my teachers that during any evening the time interval between visits to the lavatory for any individual decreases in an exponential way, while the overall frequency of visits by the entire company of assembled revellers itself increases exponentially.

Needing a pee myself, I too slipped outside to make use of the hall's toilets, which were accommodated in a separate outbuilding. To my surprise the toilet was empty but on the grass around the hall cigarette ends glowed and dimmed like tiny red fireflies as little groups of two or three clustered to the murmur of quiet conversation. After relieving myself, I strolled over – actually enjoying a break in the cooler air of the evening after the fug of the body-filled hall.

'You'll be needing a dram after all that singing,' offered Davie, pinching out his smoke and passing me an open bottle of Whyte & Mackay (for some reason the local preference in hooch).

'No,' I replied, 'you're fine – but thanks, Davie.'

He shrugged companionably and reached to place the bottle back in a niche within the stone wall which formed the boundary between the hall and my own tup field. As I looked around me in the moonlight I realised that each man had a bottle, clearly secreted in advance in preparation for the long evening ahead, and each man replaced his bottle in a separate cache within the wall before drifting back to the hall in their ones and twos. This, then – and not full bladders – explained the comings and goings taking place so discreetly as the evening passed by. Grinning quietly to myself, I also returned to the hall – the door held open for me by some new escapee – and reclaimed my seat.

THE FACTOR'S BULL

The Laird had a reputation for a somewhat short fuse, and while Dolly and the ever-versatile handyman, John Angus, were lifers inherited from The Aunt it seemed that shepherds and farm managers did not stay long before some ruction would lead to their dismissal or resignation. Perhaps the Laird had mellowed somewhat by the time I knew him, but I always suspected that this irascibility was based on uncertainty and frustration and the responsibility of managing a large Estate he had not asked to inherit on behalf of a wider family trust of himself and his two brothers.

Big Estates like Lochuisge pose a host of problems in the management of their day-to-day affairs – and simply gobble up money. Before the days of micro-hydroelectric schemes or windfarms to boost revenues, most Highland Estates were run at a very significant loss – with an average deficit across the various Estates for which I have worked of the order of £100,000 a year. The general rule of thumb was then that an Estate would cost you in every year around 10 per cent of its initial purchase price – and even now they can at best hope to 'wash their face' (or break even). There are costs associated with maintenance of roadways, and maintenance of buildings and farms, and costs most heavily associated with employment of staff to run the place: farm staff, stalkers and ghillies, staff for the House. While many modern commentators offer strong criticism of an outdated feudalism implicit in private ownership of large Estates, the Estates were for the most part the major employers for a wide surrounding area where there was little other work to be had, and played a key role in enabling many remote Highland communities to survive both socially and economically. Without the Estate many would have drifted to the towns; whole villages and communities in these more rural areas would have disappeared as surely as in the Clearances. Our Laird at least believed in Belloc's maxim that 'it is the duty of the wealthy man to provide employment to the artisan'. But our Laird was perhaps not so wealthy, and I suspect that much as he loved it, the burden of the Estate – and its parlous economics – weighed heavily on his shoulders, so that at times of frustration even minor setbacks would assume inflated and even nightmarish proportions and appear as the final straw, releasing an ill-considered reaction and a fiery temper; at all events he did not seem to keep either stockmen or factors for long.

I never did work out Sandy's real position; in effect he played the role of factor (or Estate manager) from a safe distance; never resident on the Estate. The Estate bull was becoming old – and in any case had been within the herd for long enough now that many of the cows to be serviced were his own daughters. Gone were the days of the Department Bull, a peripatetic stud animal provided by the Department of Agriculture, which did the rounds of each local area, walked from hamlet to hamlet to service the cattle of the crofters too poor, or with too few beasts, to justify maintaining their own bull; and Lochuisge's herd was in any case too large to be reliant on the Department Bull or the techniques of artificial insemination which had finally displaced it. Time was to find a new and younger bull for the Estate herd.

Sandy had heard of some suitable animals available back beyond the ferry port and some 100 miles away to the south: beef shorthorns from a herd with reputation. Perhaps short of time, he did not check for himself, but dispatched the (equally new) young shepherd to go and collect the chosen beast – a young animal selected, it would appear, on the basis of its bloodline and not a proven sire; knowing the Laird, cost probably had something to do with it as well. Young Donald duly returned, and a fine young Adonis of a bull it was, to be sure, that cautiously descended the aluminium ramp of the cattle float to survey his new home: a glossy white shorthorn with curly poll and fine physique. A physique of which he was clearly only too proud, himself; for over the weeks ahead, while posing imposingly among his cows, he covered not a single one, although he showed a remarkable interest in the young bullocks in the adjacent field. Too late the penny dropped that this was one of those rare animals, a genuinely gay bull; he was returned with alacrity to his former owners, and a replacement, however less imposing, was quickly procured.

It was the talk of the peninsula in the District Agricultural Show a fortnight later. In many ways the Show was the highlight of the social year. So many of the local people were farmers or crofters and at the very least had a few livestock; at the same time so many of them lived in remote farms and croft-houses in isolated parts of the peninsula that they perhaps saw little of each other except when passing in town or at the livestock sales. But the Show was where they could let their hair down a little, share a beer and catch up with some of the gossip, reminding themselves and each other of some of the year's events; all of it old news and well rehearsed, but brought out again and dusted off to be discussed again with new listeners. The Show also had its more serious side in that each could show off a little and display their skills as stockmen and breeders of the finest livestock. The Laird and the wealthier local farmers spruced up and decked themselves in their best tweeds for the occasion; the crofters perhaps cared less about their own appearance of patched trousers and holed jerseys, but devoted equal time to primping and preening their livestock. Cattle were washed and brushed till their coats gleamed; hooves and horns were oiled and polished. The blackface tups too had their corkscrew horns oiled till they shone, their fleeces shampooed and tinted with a hint of colour. (This practice had begun some years earlier in advance of stock sales, in order to distract the eye, perhaps, from underlying blemishes in the quality or the kemp of the wool; however, as soon as one person does it, the practice is quickly followed, as everyone else seeks to conceal the imagined failings of their own stock. Before long a level playing field is restored because all are at the same game – but thereafter all the sheep must sport dyed fleeces for the occasion.)

Our showground was at the other end of the peninsula on coastal flats overlooking the wide sea loch. One could hardly imagine a more spectacular backdrop of rugged peaks behind the ruffled water of the loch itself. Around a central ring cordoned off with ropes were erected a motley array of tents and small marquees to house the trade stands, the plant sales of cuttings and plantlets from the garden of the Big House, local arts and crafts and a large produce tent. Away to one side were hurdled enclosures for the sheep and cattle – curiously and, surely coincidentally, more or less next door to the beer tent. A separate small tent housed the smaller cages for bantams and laying hens, ducks and other fowl, largely shown by the children. There was a tent devoted wholly each year to a competition for stick dressing,[22] and another area set aside for displays by the local volunteer fire brigade. After the stock judging and the withdrawal of those successful or less successful to celebrate or commiserate in the beer tent, the main ring hosted the usual concourse of vintage tractors, then perhaps a display of flying by the local falconer or a display of the local pack of fell-hounds by the houndsman.[23]

This latter display, while always very popular, always descended into total chaos since our much-loved local houndsman always appears to have limited control over his exuberant charges. The afternoon always drew to a close with the ritual terrier racing when the equally undisciplined terriers of the local stalkers and ghillies were encouraged to run after a mechanical lure; given the cantankerous nature of most of the competitors however, this usually degenerated rapidly into a melee of fairly good-natured dogfights and a flurry of owners trying to disengage their particular prize-fighter. The beer tent finally disgorged its boozy contents for the final traditional tug-of-war before all dispersed, albeit a little unsteadily. Later in the evening the organisers would somewhat optimistically hold what became known as the Survivors' Dance.

Each year, in addition, a more modest shearing and stock-judging competition was held at one of the local farmsteads. While

---

22 preparing and whipping handles of wood or dressed ramshorn to sticks and shepherd's crooks

23 In Scotland, while hunting to hounds has long been illegal, it is still permitted to run a pack of foothounds to flush hill foxes from their dens among standing cairns of hill stones, to standing guns. Many local communities operate such packs and may share the huntsman.

initially this had circulated from farm to farm, over the years it had more or less assumed a fixed home in the sheds and farmyard of one of our neighbours. By this time in the year Johnny would have finished clipping his tups and the majority of his older ewes before reuniting them with their lambs. But he always kept back a pen of a hundred or so hoggs (yearling females) for the competition. And out in the yard were hurdled pens of calves or heifers, lambs and shearlings, in trios or fours, all colour-labelled for the assembled company to judge. These had previously been ranked for their quality by an independent judge, and the aspiring competitor whose rankings came closest to those determined beforehand would carry off the trophy. In fact the outcome was probably as random as the raffle; the guest judges in most years had little or no knowledge of livestock and were as likely as not to have ranked the animals on the basis of their prettiness than their commercial quality.

The shearing competitions took place in Johnny's big open barn. Spectators sat on pallets or on the big sacks of wool from the ewes clipped earlier in the summer, stuffed full and stitched closed. Swallows skimmed overhead through the open doors to their nests in the rafters. Although everyone joined in the fun, the clipping competitions were taken surprisingly seriously.

Competitions were both for machine shearing with electric clippers and for more traditional hand-held shears. I loved this annual competition, watching it by lounging on an overstuffed woolsack in the cool, airy barn; somehow with its local focus, it meant so much more than the televised competitions between world champions. Our boys were skilled – and knew their sheep.

Each pair of shearers would enter the arena and stand by their appointed post beneath two shearing machines suspended from the rafters by corded baler twine. Helpers would shed a parcel of six hoggs into small pens and these 'croggers' would thereafter catch and feed to the shearer a replacement beast each time the fleece of the previous animal was clipped and rolled. At the off, each clipper would go to his pen and sheep, and receive a beast from the crogger; deftly turning the animal onto its back with a single twist he would lift it back to the plywood board resting below his clipping machine and sit it neatly upright on its buttocks. Never taking his eyes off the sheep, his hand would snake upwards and tug the dangling cord which started the motor of the electric clippers. The fleece would be opened with a single swift stroke upwards across the chest and up into the neck, clearing the neck wool from the teeth of the clippers with a deft flick, and then without a pause the clippers would skim over the shoulders and down over the ribs, with gentle repeated strokes as the creamy clean underwool was exposed beneath the stained surface of the outside of the fleece. Each shearer wore soft felt moccasins and the animal was rocked to and fro by gentle movements of the feet to reposition it as clipping progressed down towards the haunches and the tail. The chattering teeth of the electric clippers reached up over the spine and the process was repeated down the opposite flank. While some hoggs might offer token resistance and a few kicks, they were held firm by the knees and strong hands of the shearers and indeed most of the animals bore the whole process with remarkable calm. From this it was clear that the skill of the shearer was not just in the actual shearing but in the firm but gentle series of holds on the sheep, so that it would almost seem to be dancing with him.

The final strokes parted the sheep from its wool, and with the fleece now on the floor each shearer would return the freshly shorn animal to his personal pen for close examination by the judges. Picking up and shaking out the fleece onto its back, he would now flick in the sides towards the middle and quickly roll the fleece from tail to neck; the neck wool would be twisted into a strong rope and wrapped to secure the bundle tightly with a single jerk of the wrist, before the fleece was tossed aside and the shearer went back to the pen to collect his next partner. The newly shorn hoggs, released and supposedly herded back into to the pens, occasionally missed their path and rampaged through the seated ranks of onlookers much to general delight, because this would cost time points.

Proceedings were watched over by eagle-eyed judges who patrolled among the machines, and checked the animals returned to the catching pens, awarding points based on the quality of the clipping, speed and awarding penalty points for any minor nicks to the animal's hide – although in fairness, our shearers were very careful and rarely clipped so close as to cause a cut to the skin. Points were also awarded for the quality of roll and the tightness of the rolled fleece. For some reason it is traditional that fleeces from Scottish blackface sheep are rolled with the outside of the fleece on the outside and the creamy underwool curled inside, while those for Cheviots or cross-breds are rolled outside in. It is a convention I have never fully understood – but I confess that when helping with the clipping of the mixed flocks on the Lochuisge Estate, where not uncommonly I drew the short straw of rolling fleeces, this difference kept me on my toes and I frequently got myself muddled.

While surely competitive, and everyone took it all very seriously, there was a light-heartedness about the day which meant that all were happy enough whoever won the competitions. Perhaps this was in part due to the fact that sheep-clipping at Johnny's was always enlivened by the appearance of Grampa's van. Grampa had a day job (although I never discovered quite what it was) but spent his weekends touring the local country shows and events dispensing chips and gravy, venison burgers, wisecracks, gin and whisky in equal measure in a seamless, continuous flow. It is the first and only burger van I have known which offered not only beef and venison burgers, with the requisite and ubiquitous gallons of tea, but also had a row of optics secured to the back wall, dispensing whisky, gin, vodka (and the ladies' favourite: peach schnapps). Milk for the tea was in an old ketchup bottle (where else?). Grampa was something of a one-off and did a roaring trade – in part because of the endless stream of wisecracks, usually well-targeted; a local himself, he knew everyone there and thus the jokes were sometimes pretty carefully pointed. My problem is that I can never remember those barbed humoresques even only a few hours' later – but Grampa was a trouper, and with all the alcohol that flowed so freely, it never ceased to amaze me that hoggs clipped at the end of the competition emerged as well shorn as those earlier on in the proceedings.

SHEEPDOG TRIALS

The other main event of the farming year – or rather, the other main social event – was the annual chance for the local shepherds to display their skills in the local sheepdog trials. These were traditionally held at the very neck of the peninsula near the showground, on a fine open (and from our point of view, unusually flat) piece of ground on Iain Cameron's farm at Ardness. Just as competitive in its way as the clipping competition, the rivalry, while serious, was equally light-hearted, as each of the shepherds showed off their skills at training and handling their dogs – and, just as importantly, paraded the quality of those working collies.

Grampa's van would again be in attendance, and on a sunny day it was always a relaxed and convivial occasion. While ostensibly local, in fact competitors came from miles around to compete, so that it must have been viewed as something more of a regional event. Jimmy Urquhart came over with his dogs from Knoydart (having taken the earliest possible ferry); Andy the haulier – who delivered to all of us hay harvested over on the more predictable East Coast – travelled over for the day from Thornhill near Stirling; others too came from far enough afield – but they were regulars, and all had in addition some previous link with Lethinnis to draw them back as honorary locals. And unquestionably the main rivalry was amongst the local crofters and the shepherds of the big Estates; Lochuisge, Saimhairidh, Ardslignish. The main distinction perhaps from 'show' competitions was that these were not show dogs, brought up primarily for trialling: these were all working dogs, bred and trained for long hours of hard work gathering half-wild sheep from the huge expanse of outrun on the open hill, but now being tested for their skills under these more controlled conditions. And on a sunny day it was a spectacular location, with the long open field backed by the sparkling waters of the loch.

We always went for the fun of it – and for the 'craic' – but I confess I myself was always more impressed by the control I would see these same men having with their dogs working the open hill – with the dog maybe as much as half a mile away on the opposite hillside, or even out of sight over some ridge – where the measure of the skill and the close understanding between shepherd and dog would reveal itself by the sudden appearance of a group of sheep on the top of that same distant ridge, spilling over steadily and unhurriedly to join the cluster of animals already ahead of us on the hill track, with the tireless collie perhaps appearing as much as a minute or two later. With the best dogs you never had to go and check whether they had missed any or let any slip back behind, and they worked as much from instinct and long training as in obeying any immediate commands from a master who could trust them and could not, in many cases, see where they were anyway. I was a veteran of such hill gathers, but the skill and initiative – and sheer stamina – of those dogs never failed to astonish me. Ours was steep ground, and the dogs must have covered mile after mile at considerable speed, yet the best of them could work all day, and it was only the older dogs who would need a substitute brought on later in the gather as we got closer to the home pens and handling yards.

But today was more for show. Andy went first, sending his bitch Moss way out along the far fence for a clean pick-up of his allotted parcel of ewes, and bringing them through the first gateway, round a distant marker post back through a second gateway. A whistle dropped the collie dead in her tracks to hold the little group of animals stationary on open ground. One of the ewes was sporting a red ribbon around her horn; Moss cut into the heart of the little group, which scattered before her, shedding out the marked sheep and separating her from the rest before quickly reassembling the remaining animals into a tight bunch and moving them on again towards the final pen.

Holding the makeshift gate open with one hand and stretching out his crook to make a larger barrier, Andy whistled the collie on. But she was too keen and too close: the sheep came on too fast and scattered, some going into the pen but others overshooting down its far side. Points lost. All the spectators groaned in sympathy as Andy walked around the outside of the pen to herd those animals within it outside again and be rounded up once again with their fellows by a somewhat chastened Moss. The gate was opened wide again, and Andy's crook outstretched; this time Moss did not crowd so close, but slowly nudged the sheep forward with that delightful creeping half-crouched gait that collies can command. And this time the gate closed on a full pen.

Then there was a roar of laughter from the direction of Grampa's van: obviously one of his sneaky little quips had struck home again at someone's abashed expense, as Jimmy took his collie to the field to test his mettle. And with piercing whistles, and shouts of 'Come by', 'Away to me' and the more urgent cries of 'Lie down, damn you!' (in such context we knew of a man whose collie was known to all as 'Bob-you-bastard,' because his name was never called without the addition of the accompanying epithet) the afternoon wore on.

This afternoon, the competition was going to come from Davie and his little wall-eyed bitch, Jill. Davie was one of the four shepherds at Ardslignish, a gentle, self-effacing man with a definite taste for a dram – and wee Jill was something special. Both master and dog were small, wiry and intelligent, and at 60-odd Davie had had a lifetime's shepherding. With his eyes screwed up more against the spiral of smoke from his roll-up than from the brightness of the day, Davie strolled out onto the display field, Jill glued to his feet. The buzz of chatter actually quietened because everyone knew that this was the team to beat. Jill hardly needed commands, she knew her job so well, and she was so slight she almost flew over the ground; if she had a failing at all it was that she could at times be almost too fast. Everybody stopped to watch: a clean pick-up, swiftly through those first gates and round the turn post. Jill dropped flat as the little flock of sheep slowed to a halt and bunched anxiously in a tight group. At Davie's shrill whistle she cut through the group and shed the ribboned ewe before quickly circling and closing the remainder once more into a tight group and bringing them slowly through the next set of gates towards the final pen. Davie wasn't going to repeat Andy's mistake and kept Jill as far back as he dared, relying on her 'eye' to keep the sheep moving forward … but was it going to be fast enough? He urged her closer, but the little group of ewes started to look much more anxious and skittish, so she dropped back again of her own accord. Jill held the group still as Davie opened the gate and stretched out his stick – and then they were in and the gate closed. But it had been slow, and we could see Iain Cameron, as judge, shaking his head.

At the end of the day it was a draw, but no one really cared – and least concerned of all was Davie.

A DAY OUT ON TRESHNISH

While the car ferry to town was 42 miles away back up the road, Lochuisge had always had a closer association with Scarpay than the mainland, and once a week a local boatman operated a weekly passenger service across the water to Scarpay's main town of Kilmory. Things of course tended to be a lot more expensive at island prices, but if you took into account the cost of the mileage and the car ferry to town, then it was more equable and in any case most of us who travelled saw it as an outing. The reinstatement of the ferry service, which had been discontinued long ago, had in any case been something of a community enterprise, with refurbishment of the stone slipway and installation of a floating walkway operational at higher tides, when the main slipway was underwater.

The forecast was good, and Ewan the ferryman had felt like a day off, so had phoned round a number of locals proposing an outing through the Cairns of Coll and on down to the Treshnish Isles, just as a 'jolly'. Suddenly essential chores for the day ahead seemed less urgent and could clearly be postponed for a later juncture as the village got itself prepared for a picnic. At the appointed hour nearly the entire community was out waiting above the slipway, and in fairness it was only about an hour later that we heard the sounds of the powerful diesel engines, and *Cathula* appeared around the point.

It was high tide, so Ewan throttled back the engines and moored the boat to the floating landing stage moored in the bay beforehand,

and nosed her gently against the rocks of the shore for everyone to scramble aboard.

It is a long pull around the north tip of Mull through the Cairns of Coll with their basking seals and down the West Coast; *Cathula*'s sturdy engines – and indeed her own body shape – were built for stamina not speed; but there is always something to watch on a boat and the conversation never languished. Ewan's wife, Alison, brought frequent mugs of tea from the forward galley. Despite the apparent leisured pace of life in this part of the Highlands, we all actually worked hard – long hours, and for the most part hard physical work – so that a day off such as this was actually a relatively rare pleasure, to be savoured to the full.

Resplendent as ever in his trademark yellow wellies, Ewan was a knowledgeable and experienced seaman and a keen amateur naturalist, so that the journey passed pleasurably as we kept an eye out for porpoises and dolphins and perhaps the (rather rarer) glimpse of a basking shark or orca. Eventually we rounded the tip of Caliach Point and could see Treshnish in the distance. The Treshnish Isles are a group of uninhabited islands off the west coast of Mull, dominated by the larger islands of Fladda and Lunga and – jutting out far to the west – the distinctive outline of the Dutchman's Cap – well named, for in its shape it looks so much like the winged cap of the traditional Dutch bonnet (or to my eye, the very similar outline of a folded paper sailing boat). Lower-slung Lunga, though closer, emerges more slowly, but eventually we nosed into the bay and dropped anchor.

At that time privately owned, Lunga, like the other islands in the group, is uninhabited – at least by humans – but is a sanctuary for seabirds, with big resident colonies of nesting puffins, razorbills and guillemots. In general these are (or were) relatively undisturbed so that the nesting birds were ludicrously approachable. Many more local boatmen now take tourist trips to the island – in vessels faster than *Cathula* – so that it is more difficult to have the place to oneself; but there is an upside even to that increased disturbance. Foraging puffins and guillemots returning from far out to sea with beakloads of sand eels and other small fish for their nesting partners and chicks regularly had to run the gauntlet of attack by marauding gulls and hooded crows as they approached the shore, often losing their catch of fish to the continued harassment. But now, adjusting to the increased frequency of human visitors to the island, the returning auks often wait at sea for the arrival of the next batch of humans before they themselves come ashore, because the gulls and hooded crows are more wary of humans than are the auks, and the presence of the tourists discourages the gulls and crows to an extent from intercepting and bullying the puffins and guillemots as they fly in with their sand eels.

Lunga had – and still has – no jetty or pier, so that access to the island was restricted to the more able-bodied of *Cathula*'s passengers; we swarmed over the side into the boat's tender – a rubber dinghy – which ferried us in relays to the shingle of the beach. Here we were greeted by the cloying stench of guano intermixed with the smell of rotting seaweed, an aroma which intensifies as one wades ankle-deep across the saltmarshes of the inner shore and through the accumulated tangle of wrack towards the foot of the central plateau. The smell is indescribably awful but the journey is mercifully short to reach the steep sandy climb to the turf-covered plateau.

This is classic maritime cliff vegetation: a dense sward of short turf interspersed with sea-holly, drifts of wild thyme, harebells and sea-thrift, the sward kept short through the grazing activity of hundreds of rabbits, whose burrowing in the sandy hilltop also provides whole council estates for breeding puffins. And the puffins were everywhere. It pulls me up short every time how small they are in reality and how totally delightful, with their black and white frock-coats and brightly-enamelled beaks. The smudge of makeup around their eyes and their apparent inability to master anything other than a crash-landing, makes them appear so comical, but in practice these are hard-working and earnest little birds who always seem busy. And there is something intensely pleasing about the continuous buzzing chatter of the dense-packed colony. Each time I visit Lunga, I linger on this short stretch of close-cropped turf for hours among the puffins and the harebells.

But Lunga is an island of clear demarcations and ethnic enclaves. This is puffin-town, but within a short walk it is left behind and you are walking through less densely packed suburbs populated by the occasional razorbills who do not seem to like their neighbours quite that close. Here the black-backed gulls and hoodies are more in evidence, and under that cairn of jumbled rocks an aggressive hissing and wide green gape reveals the nest of a shag, its iridescent green feathers almost invisible in the gloom of the crevice. Cross a rocky arête, and suddenly you are thrust into the middle of an extensive colony of common guillemots. We may have travelled less than half a mile from the puffin colony, but their close-cropped turf is now replaced by sheer, naked rock, where thousands of common and brindled guillemots jostle for position, each guarding a single egg laid on the narrowest ledge of rock. The noise and the smell should be appalling, but in fact the whole experience is somehow uplifting as one takes in the immensity of the clustered jostling horde of nesting birds so densely packed together. It is a constant commotion, an ever-seething mass of birds in constant motion as they seek to maintain position within the throng.

As always I have tarried too long. But no one minds. By the time I return, most of the other passengers are back on the shore. Ewan has somehow managed to tranship even the less able-bodied from *Cathula*, together with an array of picnic baskets and is presiding over a driftwood fire on the shingle, barbecuing sausages. The smell of cooking even threatens to swamp that of guano and rotting seaweed. The day has stayed fine as forecast; *Cathula's* more regular employment – and Ewan's – is to take out day trips, sea-fishing, and as we chug gently home, Ewan hands round rods to those who want them and we troll over the stern for mackerel in the failing light. More in idle relaxation than in earnest, but who knows: the outing may yet provide food for the morrow as well.

APRIL SHOWERS AND MAY FLOWERS

John slammed in the final staple and put down the wire tensioners. He straightened his back. It had taken us most of the morning to put up that section of the fence, but now the fresh galvanising of the netting glittered in the sun. We had been busy when time could be spared from other routine daily tasks, refencing and extending the tup field beside the hall ready to separate the lusty males from the ewes and their new lambs. April was indeed, as T.S. Eliot intimated, the cruellest month ... but not in terms of inclement weather. While, it is true, the sun rarely shone, at least the rain had shifted more towards periodic showers rather than the incessant downpours of winter. But we all had a long list of jobs to be done in April, when the combination of the longer days and the ground beginning to dry out a little from winter's quagmire allowed one to crack on with some of the urgent outside repairs and refurbishment – before the arrival of the midges in May made such jobs once more intolerable or at the very least unpleasant. We all learnt to tolerate, to a degree, the annual emergence of the West Coast midge and its torment over the main months of summer, but the pressure was always on to get as much finished in April as we could before it became prudent to restrict outside tasks to the shortest duration practicable.

Many will claim, with bravado, that over the years you tend to become inured to the bites of the Highland midge and that you develop some sort of immunity to the torment of wearing around your face and hands a permanent cloud of black, biting insects. They lie. The bites itch interminably and no one can 'become inured' to the raids of crack squadrons of insects who seem intent on suicide missions, determined to drown themselves in the corners of your eyes, or suffocate you if only sufficient can fly together into your nostrils. I have never got used to it – and indeed each winter seem to forget a little, just how irritating are the months from May to September.

But at least the tup field was securely netted, and in the meantime our wives had been cutting back the encroaching blackthorn, whose suckering roots were inexorably invading across the open field in an advancing wave of scrub. We were perhaps less than concerned about this, but John and Judy wanted to share the grazing and put their Shetland ponies into the same paddocks. We donned thicker gloves and went to help to drag some of the dry but thorny stems into a pile as a core for a fire to be burnt later that same week. The field had also become infested with bracken, but I had already sprayed herbicide on half the previous summer, and was preparing to brave the midges and attack the second half in a dry spell in June if one might ever materialise. (By then I might have become more accustomed to the midges again – and with a bit of luck might choose a breezy day when onshore winds might keep them more at bay.)

A couple of days later, time and conditions were just right to have that bonfire and clear the field just in time to put the tups across. It had stayed dry and there was no real wind to fan the flames to an excessive heat. Young Seamus materialised as if from nowhere (the 10-year-old loved a good bonfire), so with him in tow, more for moral support than actual assistance, I set off with newspaper and matches to see if we could get the fire to go. For once it lit quickly and with minimal fuss, so I left Seamus in charge and set off to and fro across the field dragging in more and more of the dry branches. The fire burnt with an intense heat, and a ring of dry bracken fronds around its base smouldered as little licks of flame spread slowly outwards. But for the most part the density of dry fronds was not sufficient to sustain the flames, and where they took more of a hold Seamus quickly beat the spreading fire out with the back of a shovel. That was part of the fun, after all.

The flames rose higher and we were told afterwards the fire was clearly visible across the water on Scarpay. And then, without warning, the wind got up. Suddenly a well-contained fire started to spread more rapidly through the dry bracken littered across the entire field. Worse still, the wind was coming off the shore and thus the fire was spreading rapidly towards the road; already clouds of smoke were choking their way through the fringing trees and across the narrow strip of tarmac. Fortunately we were close to the end of the 42-mile trek to Lochuisge and with only a few houses beyond, there was likely to be little traffic. The flames licked closer and closer to the field margin and the new fence, on such a broad front that Seamus and I were hard put to beat it out. Each time we extinguished one front and left it to go and attend to another starting up a few metres beyond, the intense heat all around would cause the original stretch to flare up afresh. I have fought hill fires with the fire brigade, but there, although one might wish to extinguish it completely, it is usually sufficient to take control of the direction of burn and then let the flames burn themselves out harmlessly in their own time; here we had little choice but to try and hold the entire front edge of the fire before it jumped the road.

And then, when the fire was less than perhaps 3 metres from the road, just entering the fringing rows of trees, the wind turned and dropped as suddenly as it had risen and the fire died in its own ashes. Seamus and I were sweating profusely – not just from the heat of the fire and our exertions – and each was covered with a film of fine grey ash streaked in the perspiration on our faces; we must have looked a sight.

But it is an ill wind indeed that blows no good at all; and in fact the vagaries of that onshore wind had, at the end of it, set a fine fire which had cleansed the bulk of the whole field of bracken and other litter (as well as disposing of our piles of cut blackthorn). Within a few weeks, the field was a mass of flowers: bluebells nodding gracefully among the remaining areas of blackthorn, the open field a glory of orchids and globeflowers that I had never known were there, or at least had never been apparent in previous springs, perhaps suppressed by the thick underlayer of moss and dead litter. It was a spectacle almost akin to the blossoming of the machair, the short and herb-rich turf of the

Hebridean shoreline, erupting all at once into a continuous carpet of vivid blossom. I did spray the bracken, but we never tried burning that field again.

CAMAS 'INAS

Lethinnis is a patchwork of deep fjords or sea lochs incised deep into the land, with a rocky coastline of stones and seaweed-strewn shingle. As the oppressive weight of the ice sheets which covered the land in the last Ice Age has lifted, so the whole of the north of Scotland has risen out of the sea. The raised beaches of the coastal strip are fringed with woods of oak and hazel, interspersed with small cultivated fields carved out in this narrow strip of fertility. Behind it, the ground rises to a series of series of ridges and low hills. It is a beautiful place, perhaps especially so in spring and autumn, when warm days and cold nights lead to temperature inversions and a world upside-down, where the dawn breaks to thick drifts of cloud hanging low over the loch and beribboning the lower hillsides, while the higher slopes escape above the mist in the morning light.

Immediately offshore are numerous flat-topped islets, or skerries, which had in the past supported extensive colonies of sea-ducks and terns. Sadly, however, American mink have more recently invaded the peninsula, spreading north over the years from the abandoned fur farm in Appin, keeping to the coast – and devastating the offshore breeding colonies of ground-nesting seabirds. Now the skerries are used only as haul-outs by the coastal otters and the abundant seals. It was relatively rare to see the smaller common seals (or harbour seals) out of the water, and more usual to encounter their small cat-like faces bobbing upright in the water in the bay, but the large and Roman-nosed grey seals loved to bask on the rocks, head and tail ends lifted like gigantic grey bananas.

It was the Laird's proud boast that Lochuisge could flaunt six or seven different species of orchids, often with five or more all together within the space of a few square metres. Certainly in the late spring the rough marshy pastures were transformed with dense swathes of early purple orchid, northern march orchid, fragrant orchis and both greater and lesser butterfly orchid. Twayblades and helleborines too abounded along the edges of the sheep tracks.

Lochuisge was also one of the few places on the British mainland where had been recorded *Spiranthes romanzoffiana* – Irish lady's-tresses. This to, my mind rather unremarkable little flower occurs in Europe only in Ireland and the north-west of Scotland, although it is widespread throughout North America. If somewhat unprepossessing in appearance, it is indeed remarkable in other regards. It is often under-recorded because it has three distinct phases: flowering, non-flowering and a dormant underground phase in which it may rest for many years. Thus its appearance even in known sites is erratic, and it is hard to estimate its abundance because one can never be sure within any colony how many plants may still persist in that underground phase.

It is also uncertain whether or not the species established itself in Scotland comparatively recently or may have survived the last great Ice Age in ice-free refugia in Hebridean islands such as Colonsay, Coll and Barra (where it still persists) and recolonised more widely thereafter.

Its presence at Lochuisge is recorded only because one of the previous owners of the neighbouring Ardslignish Estate had been an enthusiastic amateur botanist of some considerable reputation and ability. In his botanical forays around Lethinnis he had discovered at least five distinct sites where the plant was well-established and flowered, albeit erratically. One of these was at Allt na Mhuillin, but although we found occasional specimens of narrow-leaved helleborine, we never spotted Spiranthes in any of our fields. In truth we might have missed them, given that individual plants can spend up to six years in that elusive underground phase, but during our time there, a series of skilled botanists came to re-survey the sites located by the Ardslignish

Laird and search for new colonies, but never found them. I had a long correspondence with one of these experts, well-familiar with the plant from his native Colonsay. Little is known about the ecology of Spiranthes and its ecological requirements; it is well-established that it is subject to local extinctions across all known sites (and sudden emergence in new sites elsewhere) and thus it is possible that a proportion of Lochuisge's known colonies had simply exhausted their reserves and died out. However, there was a lingering, if apocryphal, tale about one of the colonies in Camas Inas. Irritated with being pestered incessantly by the Ardslignish Laird and his various friends to show them where on the croft the orchid was flowering, it is rumoured that the irascible Mrs Davie uprooted the offensive specimen from her field and flung it into the sea.

A formidable character by all accounts, Mrs Davie had survived her husband Davie Cameron for many years and managed the extensive croft on her own. She had died some years before our arrival at Lochuisge, and her bow-fronted cottage, at the end of the curving row in Camas Inas, had now been sold on as a holiday cottage. In its past the curve of the bay had housed its own independent community, with half a dozen houses and a smithy. Everywhere were signs of long occupation, with charcoal-burners' huts and kilns scattered amongst the oak and hazel woods along the coast. At some point in its history, a low wall had been built across one arm of the bay, submerged at high tide, but exposed by the receding water: this had served the community for many years as a fish trap, with shallow-water species swimming in with the tide to be trapped behind the half-wall as the water fell. But nowadays Camas Inas was largely undisturbed, and the focus of human occupation had shifted to Sealach na Mara and Lochuisge, further along the coast. A couple of sailing boats now found moorings over the summer months in the bay and otherwise it was a largely tranquil spot.

But it was far from unoccupied. Camas Inas was a haven for otters: the stubby, grassy promontories sticking out into the water were pockmarked with muddy tracks worn deep into the short turf providing evidence of decades of use to be worn so deep. At the margins were steep mudslides where generations of otters had slipped into the sea, and there were slides over the rocks, polished smooth by the passage of hundreds of lithe bodies across the years. It was a commonplace to see the otters themselves foraging along the shoreline or bobbing just offshore, watching from the safety of the kelp beds.

As in many parts of northern Scotland, particularly in the west, otters were still common and while they would travel inland up the steep burns, these tended to be small and shallow – nearly dry except when in spate, so that the animals foraged largely along the coast, lying up to rest in cairns of rocks along the shoreline. They took large numbers of crabs and other shore life – especially the younger cubs who were not yet experienced foragers – but there isn't enough sustenance in a diet exclusively of crustacea and to supplement their diet they all had to hunt in addition for fish in the shallow waters of the bay. Perhaps the old fish trap at Camas Inas was a bonus for them as well.

But despite popular supposition, there is no distinction in the UK between river otters and sea otters; those living by the coast have adopted the habit secondarily and all must travel to fresh water regularly to wash the salt from their sleek fur, since if it becomes clogged with salt it loses its waterproofing. So, once a day if not more frequently, they would swim to the mouth of the river or one of the smaller burns to wash and groom; occasionally, especially if the cubs were small, they would venture further up-river and we would hear the kits calling with a high-pitched whistle if they feared they were being left behind. In winter, the otters would venture even further inland, and it was not uncommon to find otter paw-prints in the snow high up in the hills. The bolder adults would raid chicken runs, so those of us who kept fowl had to be extra vigilant.

And wherever they travelled, they would mark their territories with their droppings. Otter territories are largely linear (along the line of the coast itself, or along the line of rivers and streams) and they maintained ownership of these territories by leaving these characteristic spraints at intervals – on prominent flat rocks, under bridges, and wherever other otters might be most likely to encounter the signal saying 'this is mine'. Otter spraint is actually rather distinctively sweet-smelling, with a hint about it of jasmine tea. The larger droppings of pine martens were characteristically musky – and usually iridescent blue-black because of their preference for feeding on dung beetles, so that the scats were full of shiny purple wing-cases. Mink stink.

TOURETTE'S

The other cottage which had been sold away as a holiday home was the old ferryman's cottage around the coast at Shieldaig. It had been owned for many years by a retired surgeon from Edinburgh and his wife. Cameron was a small, rather excitable man, who spent his weekends at the cottage pottering amongst serried banks of batteries and accumulators experimenting with different designs of home-made wind and water turbines to find a way of providing the cottage with regular electricity. Joanne was a warm, generous, hospitable woman, in no way suppressed or dominated by her eminent husband – and an extraordinarily good cook.

By this time I was living on my own at Allt na Mhuillin, and Joanne had stopped by on the way out to Shieldaig the previous evening to suggest I might like to come over the following day for a bite of lunch. The day had dawned fine, so I set off early to stop at the Estate yard for a blether with John Angus before continuing along the winding coastal track which led to Shieldaig. Subject to only infrequent use since the closure of the ferry many years before, it was a narrow track, ill-maintained and with precipitous drops away to the side; it was passable only with a fairly rugged 4×4, and then only with the greatest of care. I drove cautiously over the bumpy surface, strewn with boulders from previous rock-slides from above, winding my way past derelict crofts and the long-abandoned townships of Pollochan and Portnacroish.

There was a sad air to these old townships, now reduced to piles of tumbled stones overgrown with moss, but still retaining the clear outlines of dwellings and outhouses and even a church. Now occupied only by wild hill sheep who scattered at my approach, these hamlets had once supported thriving populations: Portnacroish and the outlying cluster at Sruthain had boasted some 15 separate houses in their heyday, and this pattern had been repeated along the coast. Parish records repeated a sad litany of 'abandoned by 1871; abandoned by 1872; cleared 1855' – because all these scattered hamlets had been casualties of the infamous Clearances, when crofters and cottars were summarily evicted from their houses by the owners or factors of the big Estates, to make way for sheep. Almost always the roof timbers (a precious commodity in this land of relatively few large few trees) were removed or burnt to prevent re-occupation. But we should not get too sentimental about those Clearances, or indeed judge those who evicted cottar families by our 21st-century morals or mores. The poorer people living off the land had few rights in those long-distant days – and while indeed many of the evictions were callously and cruelly carried out, in reality, however romantic one would wish to be, how many of these remote hamlets *would* still be occupied today had no Clearances occurred? From generations of cropping, the poor soils of those small areas which could support a meagre crop of oats or potatoes were poorer each year. There was no electricity. Water had to be carried. Life was hard, and modern expectations of a colour television, dishwasher and a smart motor car would surely have ensured the death of remote crofting communities in any case, as the younger folk moved away, tempted by the creature comforts and regular employment in the towns. Even today, there is a steady drift of young people away from rural communities to find work in the towns and cities. I am in no way defending the manner of the Clearances, but it is perhaps important not to get too dewy-eyed about the emptying of the land.

The track descended through a patch of scrubby birch and down into Shieldaig.

Cameron met me in the yard. 'Have you got them?' he blurted.

'Have I got what, exactly?' I asked, cautiously.

'The plants. Didn't you get my phone message?' Although the conversation was now getting dangerously repetitive, I enquired 'What phone message?'

'I left a message explaining that Kirsty-the-Post was bringing for me some vegetable plants for the garden; because she can't get along the track here, I suggested she left them with you at Allt na Mhuillin and you could bring them over since you were coming anyway. Don't you *listen* to your effing phone messages?' Cameron was getting more heated by the moment. Gently I enquired as to what time he had left his message.

'Oh … it must have been about 11 o' clock.'

I explained that by that time I had already left.

'You *can't* have done,' he assured me, 'it only takes about an hour to get here …' Patiently I explained that I had indeed left early and had stopped off at the Estate yard to talk to John Angus, incidentally getting drawn in to helping to move some big baulks of timber he was proposing to use to help shore up the wall of the old apple store, which seemed in imminent danger of collapse.

'But you *must* have got my message.' By this stage Cameron was strutting around my pickup truck like some demented bantam cock alternately kicking my tyres violently and spluttering a staccato volley of curses. I was a little discomfited; I did not know the couple that well, and it now appeared that here was a man who, after years as a senior hospital consultant completely in charge within his own controlled domain, was accustomed to getting his own way, so that perhaps he had little practice in dealing with even the most minor setback. Fortunately Joanne was observing from the window with barely-concealed mirth and summonsed me in to take a glass of chilled white wine and a delicious bowl of home-made broth while Cameron calmed himself.

He stomped off still spluttering, but had composed himself sufficiently to join us for the excellent roast chicken and all the trimmings.

I plucked up courage. 'Perhaps,' I suggested, 'we could load your quad-bike into the back of my truck after lunch and I could give you a lift back around to Allt na Mhuillin so that you could pick up those vegetable plants yourself and still get them today?'

Somewhat mollified (perhaps in part as a result of the excellent wine) he took me on a tour of the latest experimental wind turbine and then, quad-bike aboard, we left companionably for the journey back around the coast.

Back past Portnacroish and Pollochan we climbed – somehow they seemed more peaceful and less melancholy in the afternoon light with fewer echoes of times lost – until we finally descended again to Allt na Mhuillin; John Angus had not been idle, and new clean timbers now served to prop up the undercroft of the old apple store. And back at the house, there indeed were the trays of vegetable seedlings safely in the Bothy (none of us ever locked house or outbuildings; it would have been rude, suggesting distrust of our neighbours); there indeed was the light winking on the answerphone with Cameron's missed message. Content now in safe receipt of the trays of plants, he loaded them into the box on the back of the quad and waved me a cheery goodbye.

THE MAD COW OF GLEN HURICH

Kate lived some miles from Lochuisge in a little cottage at the end of Glen Hurich. She was an attractive woman in her forties, who, despite the continuing efforts of the local gamekeeper, lived alone in the remote cottage with her invalid daughter, and usually with one or more of her shiftless sons, depending on who happened to be home at the time. She had evicted her last boyfriend some years before. He was Irish and brooding and she had kicked him out for philandering; then in subsequent renovations of the cottage after his departure, she unearthed from beneath the downstairs floorboards a number of metal cases of high explosive, several lengths of fuse cord and crates of detonators, so all in all his departure would have appeared timely. Kate worked hard on the croft and undertook all the repairs and maintenance to land and buildings herself; in such spare time as she had, she created individual items of furniture in one of the sheds at the back of the cottage, using recycled materials to produce elegant oak mirrors and settles.

We always enjoyed visits to Glen Hurich; the cottage was light and welcoming, and there was always a heap of dogs piled on the settee in the bright sitting room. Kate had a real 'way' with animals – if a somewhat eccentric way. Before she herself had arrived at the cottage, a cow had broken out from one of the paddocks and vanished into the forestry; it had never been caught and roamed feral through the trees growing wilder and more wild-eyed as the years passed. It grew huge and almost like a ghost among the trees, keeping well away from human contact and the 'mad cow of Glen Hurich' as it became known, was seen only occasionally and then fleetingly. Yet, with patience and her especial aura of calm, Kate gradually established a rapport with the beast; gradually it became tamer and more trusting, of her at least, until she was in the end able to walk it back through the gate into one of her paddocks.

The first time we ourselves had met her, a couple of years later, we had arranged to buy from her a tup and, having found our way through the forest plantations to the cottage in its little clearing of fenced paddocks, had been somewhat nonplussed by the sight of a slim gypsy-ish woman sitting barefoot in the grass, with, lying stretched beside her, a large and very woolly Jacob tup, to whom she was, in all seriousness, reading poetry. Swarming around them in the fields was a multitude of black and white rabbits, white with black polka-dot Dutch markings and black ears. Children's pets escaped some years before, Kate now made no attempt to keep them in, and while they used some of the open-fronted sheds in the yard for shelter, they lived wild and had done so for generations. Occasionally she would (with some reluctance) shoot one for the pot, but otherwise they were undisturbed and had clearly done what rabbits are prone to do – and gone forth and multiplied.

By this time I had remarried, and we had been accompanied on the trip by Jessica, my just-teen stepdaughter, who was of course enchanted by this bucolic scene and the free-range rabbits. 'Oh,' she said 'if I can catch one, can I keep it?'

Kate readily agreed, and we too accepted, certain as we were that no way was a 13-year-old going to manage to catch one of these nimble bunnies with nothing but her bare hands. How wrong we were; when we returned from loading Tolly the tup into our livestock trailer, she was clutching not one, but three somewhat startled rabbits. With resignation, but in keeping with terms agreed, we bundled them into a makeshift hutch (rapidly converted from what, from its appearance, may originally have been a wooden crate for detonators) and put it in the back of the pickup alongside a delighted Jessica. We kept them and their progeny for many years. But while Kate was convinced that

Tolly had much enjoyed the apparently regular poetry readings, that is something I am afraid we did not keep up after his return to Lochuisge.

Tolly joined the rather eclectic collection of sheep we had assembled over the years: two Scottish blackface ewes, a Gotland-Shetland cross and three pure Shetlands. They doubled up in production of lambs for the freezer and as artist's models. My wife Cathy worked as a wildlife artist and animal painter – and Scottish blackface sheep were perennially popular with the tourists. In fairness, though, we never had the courage to claim their keep as an allowable deduction on tax.

Spangle and Guinevere, the two blackface ewes, had been acquired for Jessica as orphan lambs, and bottle-reared. Gwinny developed into a gentle, affectionate, if rather short-legged creature who pottered happily around our fields but would come over to have her neck rubbed or mumble on a digestive biscuit if any of the children might appear. Spangle could not have been more different. Large for a ewe, she was a brute of a beast, cantankerous, bossy and with an enormously raucous bleat. Hawthorn had a similarly unpleasant foghorn blare when displeased. She was the Gotland-Shetland cross, with a dark, tight fleece the texture of Astrakhan, but tended to be troubled badly by flies and other biting insects causing her to wail incessantly. As she grew older, in fact, this affliction grew considerably worse, whatever creams and repellents we might apply, and she would rub bald patches on her ears and around her eyes which would dry and crack into open sores; in the end it became so troubling for her that we had no alternative but to put her down. It certainly made life quieter, but it was hard to be cross with her, realising that she truly was suffering – and an aversion to biting insects is not the best of traits on the West Coast of Scotland. Bluebell and Bramble were two of the Shetlands, small and hardy (and ideal for the older sheep-keeper, as I was becoming, because they are light enough to be lifted fully off their feet with ease). Traditionally, Shetland sheep used to be plucked of their old fleece when the new wool began to rise (pushing the old fleece outwards on an annual cycle in a similar manner to the way in which milk teeth are replaced with more permanent teeth); ours got shorn with the rest.

As I got older, so I got softer – and although the main purpose of keeping the sheep was for lambs and I had been happy enough to slaughter them in my younger days, I was finding it more and more difficult to kill the finished lambs as I grew older. Perhaps we simply did not have enough. In a larger flock the lambs might have been more anonymous; ours were known as individuals and for their individual characters. Ewe lambs we tended to keep (or swap with neighbours); male lambs (castrated earlier) should have been easier, but we developed a system of swapping them with the wether lambs of equally soft-hearted neighbours. For each of us it was somehow easier to kill animals you had not yourself reared. That was how we acquired Nigel; a moorit Shetland with deformed horns who somehow we never had the heart to put in the freezer. He had arrived, courtesy of John and Judy Petherick, one afternoon while Cathy was away. I shoved him in the field, but, perhaps not unnaturally, he kept his distance from the other sheep, who were after all strangers to him. On Cathy's return with the children, he was immediately dubbed Nigel-no-friends, and Nigel he remained. Like Gwinny, he was a friendly animal who would always come over to the fence to greet one, despite the abuse we regularly had to inflict on him: one of his horns was twisted and grew inwards towards his upper jaw, so that there was a fairly frequent need to catch hold of him and remove the growing tip with a hacksaw; he was incredibly placid during such procedures and never seemed to bear a grudge afterwards.

On sunnier days, the sheep shared their fields with our eight milking goats. These had all travelled up with us from our thatched cottage in Hampshire's New Forest and had settled happily into the converted carriage-shed we used as a big open byre. All these, too, had their names and individual characters – and I freely confess I have always preferred goats to sheep. While two Anglo-Nubians and one British Toggenburg had still been only kids when we moved, we had moved four adult British Toggenburgs and one British Alpine. All these adults were Swiss-style goats with white ears and face markings; British Toggenburgs are the British adaptation of the original brown Swiss Toggenburgs, while the British Alpine, recognised as a separate breed, is in fact simply a slightly rangier black version of much the same. British goats tend to have less marked 'trousers' than their Swiss forebears (think Mr Tumnus from *The Lion, the Witch and the*

Wardrobe) and are on the whole somewhat larger, but often retain the distinctive fatty toggles on the underside of the neck. Despite their reputation for eating anything, goats are actually rather fastidious, and they simply *hate* being wet (their coats are not waterproof) so that ours would venture down to the field only on drier days. But there was something really special about seeing them strung out along the cliff-top on mild spring days, ankle-deep in bluebells and with the sun glittering off the water of the Sound of Scarpay just beyond. They knew when they were going out, and would run down ahead of us to stop at the field gate, impatient to be let into the fields beyond.

For the rest of the time, they lived contentedly in well-strawed stalls in the converted carriage-shed, which they shared each spring and summer with nesting swallows. The space readily accommodated seven spacious stalls (the twin Anglo-Nubians, Barbara and Beetlejuice, seemed happy to share, as they had done all their lives) with a separate stall at one end fitted out as a milking parlour.

There was never any need to tether the goats for milking. There was a long, low stool placed against one wall, and when released in turn from their pens, the goats would run down the central passage and jump quickly onto this milking stand. A margarine tub-full of cereal mix kept the front end busy while the human operator manoeuvred a small three-legged stool alongside the milking stand, positioned the milking pail and drew off the fresh creamy milk. Each of the goats took about three goes of being led down the passage to the milking parlour and encouraged onto the stand before they had it off pat and would run down unaccompanied; if they finished the cereal ration before the milker had finished they never fidgeted, but would simply let their eyes glaze dreamily and, after a pause, would regurgitate and calmly start to chew their cud … but woe betide you if you tried to milk them in anything but their accustomed order. Chaos would ensue as they milled about in confused perplexity over the break with routine.

It really was never a chore doing the morning and evening milking, with one's head buried into a warm, sweet-smelling flank and the rhythmic swish, swish of milk frothing into the pail. Somehow it could never be rushed; when asked how long it took her to do the milking, an old friend of mine on Shetland, who like ourselves had about nine milkers, replied: 'Well I can do it if I have to in about half an hour … but it usually takes nearer an hour!'

Our goats all had tremendous characters and over the years I had taken some slightly mischievous pleasure in testing just how outrageous were the names I might slip past the rather stuffy registration authorities of the British Goat Society. Our herd prefix, Chevrolais, was a bad enough pun in itself, but we had twin Toggenburgs christened Trouble and Squeak, twin Anglo-Nubians Barbara and Beetlejuice – and even managed to squeeze through Chevrolais Snotgurgle and her daughter Fishface. Snotgurgle was named for the predatory giant in Rien Poortvliet's famous book *Gnomes*, but indeed you should have heard the noises she made when being bottle-fed as a kid, while Fishface could have been a gurning champion with the faces she in turn pulled around the teat.

CASSIE AND COMPANY

When we arrived at Allt na Mhuillin three of the goats were still kids, and if they were to milk as adults these would need mating; some of the adults were also through to the third or fourth year of milking following previous kiddings, so if they were to continue to produce they too would need to be mated again. Whilst we had still been in Hampshire there were sufficient other goat farmers around that there was a choice of eligible sires within a few hours' drive. Up here in Lethinnis, however, there was no such luxury of option. Initially (and obviously) in the early days we had maintained the established practice of taking any nanny in season to be mated by someone else's stud male – but now the nearest available male was a 90-mile journey away (not including the ferry trip), necessitating near enough a 200-mile round trip; if we wanted more choice, or perhaps to select a male actually matching our own breeds, we might need to travel at least double that distance. After such a long period of travel, the nanny in question might have gone off the idea to a degree; more to the point, female goats only stay in heat for about 12 hours each time, so that after a long journey it was not unusual to find they were no longer in season on arrival.

We suffered in consequence a significant number of unsuccessful trips; further, the only successful mating, while restoring the mother to milk, produced only a single kid, and a male at that. We had in the past reared these for meat, but more latterly tended to destroy them at birth (while this sounds a bit heartless, there is a vast excess of males in circulation and any goat-keeper tends to need only a single male at most). But this one we kept – a large, pure white Saanen-type with an unusually delicate head who as a goatling was really rather a handsome animal. I had always admired the (very small number) of people who had trained castrate male goats to harness, and always cherished aspirations of training one myself. Now, having 'retired' (cue for hollow laughter at this point), I had in theory more time on my hands – and here was my opportunity to train a wether to harness, whether in due course to carry me around the peninsula in some fancy goat-cart, or simply to work alongside me on the croft as a more animated wheelbarrow or beast of burden. Of course it never happened, and there never was time even to think about training him, but Little Goat, as he had been dubbed (he grew enormous), had by that time become so tame and so much part of the family that he was never going to be freezer fodder.

Ongoing problems of travelling for matings forced us in the end to the decision we would have to keep our own, entire, male. We returned to the holding of Little Goat's sire in search of a suitable candidate: in my own experience it is as well always to buy billies as kids, since if hand-reared they become more tame and more tractable when adult, and a full-size male goat can otherwise be quite a handful. Merlin was a half-caste – half Saanen, half British Toggenburg – and the nearest we were going to get to a full Toggenburg sire for our herd. We ourselves tended to remove kids from their mothers soon after birth and bottle-rear them, to ensure we could then steal a share of the mother's milk and keep her milking at capacity; otherwise the milk flow tends to diminish as the demands of the growing kid also diminish. Unlike us, however, Merlin's breeder always left kids with their mother. Merlin was too old now to be transferred to bottle-feeding, and yet if we were to gain a bond with him while he was still quite young, we needed to have him back in Lochuisge as soon as possible. With her husband currently in poor health and thus overstretched herself, the breeder suggested we should take both Merlin and his mother Cassie back to Allt na Mhuillin, returning Cassie to her once Merlin was fully weaned. Not quite the plan, but there weren't many other options, so Cassie and her young son returned with us to Lochuisge.

In the meantime, if we were to keep Merlin as an adult, we needed separate accommodation for him – and at some distance from the old carriage-shed in which were housed the females and Little Goat, because the smell of billy goat quickly taints the milk. In anticipation, I had actually cleared out the ruins of the old coal store and laundry – a separate stone-built building in one corner of the policies at some distance from both house and carriage-shed, ready for refurbishment towards just such a purpose. And from being somewhat superfluous to requirement, Little Goat would now have a new role in life as companion goat, rather than leaving Merlin in solitary confinement.

In its heyday, Allt na Mhuillin had been quite a sizeable establishment. A record for the sale of the Estate from to Alice Outhwaite in 1942 reported:

Allt na Mhuilin is approached from opposite directions through two entrance gates. There is a main building with two annexes containing in total dining room, drawing room, gun room, seven bedrooms, two dressing rooms, bathroom, two w.cs, kitchen, pantry and storeroom. The outbuildings include two larders, a stable, garage, stone dog kennel, coal cellar and laundry with a copper, two stone sinks and an ironing stove.

By our time, the house had diminished and the bedrooms within the timber summerhouse extension or Bothy had been dismantled. The roof of the coal store and adjoining laundry had fallen in, and much of the stone from the supporting walls had fallen on top as the old lime mortar had perished. Any restoration attempt was to be quite an undertaking.

Painstakingly, in spare moments I worked to remove and set aside all the building stone from inside the two buildings. Much to my surprise, underneath a thick layer of leaf mould, most of the slates from the collapsed roof remained intact. Laboriously I removed each slate and graded them; in later years a good many saw renewed service in repairs to the roof of the main house. There, indeed, stood two substantial Belfast sinks and in the corner a wood-fired copper for heating water and boiling bed linen. There, too, were other treasures –

inevitably a couple more stone cannonballs from the bombardment of Lethinnis by government forces after the Jacobite rebellion, but also a curiously intricate iron trivet used in the past as a rest for the old, fire-heated flat-irons, together (if there were any doubt as to its past usage) with a couple of the old irons themselves. Although clearing the accumulated leaf mould and debris of decades was laborious work, such discoveries were incredibly cheering and immediately restored a link with the old house in its glory days when there were servants aplenty and the laundry maids would walk to and fro from the main back kitchen to the laundry to fire the copper and cleanse the linen; those same laundry or kitchen maids who, we were told (for Kirsty and Seonaid's mother had been one of them), would entertain the local lads in that same back kitchen against the rules, leaving the back window open as an escape route. I have that same trivet and those flat-irons with me to this day as something to jog those memories.

Under all the debris we unearthed good solid concrete floors. The old sinks, sadly, had to come out, but then we set to work, to build back up the old stone walls; insert new (and slightly larger) windows, reclaimed from somewhere; fit a roof and new partition doors between the former laundry and former coal house; and finally hang a pair of stable doors in each main entrance. The stone sinks sat outside and would have made wonderful troughs for bedding plants outside what now looked like a delightful, if rather small, country cottage – but for the fact that the goats would undoubtedly have eaten them. With great good timing, Merlin and Little Goat took up their adjoining residence and Cassie went home to her rightful owners.

Merlin never did get tame (we should have held out for a kid which had been bottle-reared), and indeed I do not recall that he ever fathered any kids for us (although we did make him 'available' to other local goat-keepers who, like us, had never had their own stud male). And he did smell. He was huge and hard to handle, and the whole experiment was in truth not a great success, but for the pleasure we took in the surprised looks of occasional passers-by. The presence of visitors always alerted the two, who hurried to their doorways to rest their front hooves on the lower stable door and peer out – and each time there was a precious moment of sheer disbelief on the faces of those passing, to see a pair of goats' heads, with narrowed yellow eyes, looking at them with interest over the top of identical stable doors from what appeared to be a pair of semi-detached, if somewhat diminutive, stone cottages.

GORSEFLOWER WINE

The old ostlers' quarters, accessed separately up a short flight of stone stairs at the back of the house, made an excellent winery, and once we had installed a heating system in the old house the warmth from the oil-fired boilers that were housed there made a perfect temperature for fermentation. The eventual installation of the heating was a saga in itself: as I took Tony the plumber into the builders' merchants in town for the second time to buy replacement drill bits for those worn down or broken from his attempts to bore through the old whinstones, I couldn't help but overhear his lugubrious muttering to the sales assistant: 'First time it's taken me two effing hours to drill through one effing wall …' But I digress.

I have always taken pleasure in making (and consuming) country wines. While, in the same way that it is satisfying to grow one's own fruit and vegetables, there is a certain satisfaction in making productive use of wild fruits and flowers – wasting *nothing* of the resources available; there is also, I confess, enormous pleasure to be had from the simple gathering of these same fruits and flowers, enjoying the scents and colours of the seasons, being out and somehow connected with the landscape. There is also some satisfaction in the production, after many months, of something that faithfully captures – and preserves – the smells and colours of spring and autumn. I imagine the same is true for those who use wild fruits to make jams and jellies: the translucent clarity of a well-made bramble jelly, the purple depth of colour and the flooding of the senses with the scent of autumn when one actually opens the jar – all these apply equally to a well-made wine.

Storage intensifies and translates both the aroma and the flavour. Some wines keep faithful to the original scent – thus elderflower wine does indeed smell of elderflowers – but others alter both nose and taste. Few people imagine that parsley wine once matured holds no hint of parsley but tastes like a fine hock or, with its tint of green, perhaps a fresh Soave; that after two years of storage sloe wine has the depth and volume of a fine burgundy. Joanne Harris gives some feel for this transmutation – and the magical, evocative power of a well-made wine – in her wonderful book *Blackberry Wine*; I cannot hope to emulate her prose but I do make good wine!

Over the years I have always made use of what was immediately available – or taken close note of fruiting trees and bushes perhaps further afield, but which I might pass during trips abroad; through spring there was always a clean pillowcase on the back seat of the car in case of elderflowers, and through autumn some empty buckets here and there. And in case some commodity might entail too distant (or too rare) a trip, then I have converted the garden of every house I have occupied into a winemaker's garden, planting hawthorn or blackthorn if none already exist, rooting slips of elder, planting apple orchards and plums. In Hampshire I had planted grapevines, which did surprisingly well, but then so did peaches and figs on the warm brick of a south-facing wall and I didn't imagine any of these exotics would survive or prosper in Lethinnis!

Indeed it was rare even to find elderberries there; while there were elder bushes and elderflowers in abundance, very rarely did the flowers set fruit, and then in such sparse quantities that it was insufficient for wine. But sloes there were, if you knew where to forage, and against lean years there were years where the blackthorn bushes were so laden that surplus could be put in the freezer to hedge against a future year when pickings were thin. I found recipes for wine from rowanberries – and there were always loads of these – but I confess, however long it was matured, I always found this bitter and acrid, and fully understood why naïve young pine martens would experiment with eating the abundant berries only to vomit them up again undigested. By contrast, while equally dry, home-made rice wine, or sake, was a consistent success.

Despite Joanne Harris' title choice, blackberry wine never worked well for me, even if I could beat the birds and woodmice and pick sufficient fruits in the first place. Whatever I did to adjust sugar levels, it always seemed to ferment out too sweet for my tastes and, if kept to mature longer, would commonly start a secondary fermentation in the bottle almost a year later – almost as if in sympathy with the changing seasons and the time the next year's crop of fruit was ripening; nights were punctuated with dull thumps as corks exploded from bottles and the floor of the cellar was covered with a purple sticky goo.

There were always, though, spare currants from the overgrown bushes in the abandoned orchard, although I sometimes had to be inventive with recipes and create mongrel mixtures to make up quantities. The same old orchards yielded bushels of apples of assorted varieties: these made excellent wine on their own, but, like the copious volumes of marrow wine I also fermented from overblown courgettes, proved more useful still for blending with other wines which on their own proved too acid or perhaps too full-flavoured.

In Lethinnis there is a saying that when the gorse is not in flower kissing is out of season: a safe enough assessment since somewhere, whatever the time of year there would always be a few yellow blossoms on the whins. This was another one not to waste, then – especially in the peak of the flowering in early May when the gentle scent of coconut on the air on a warm, sunny day hints at perhaps something delicately scented in the final bottling. Plucking the flowers themselves is not for the faint-hearted: whin bushes protect their blossoms well, and few extend beyond the dense spines of the stems. You need to affect the style of TV films of tea-pickers in India or Ceylon, portrayed always as beautiful Asian ladies in bright gauzy dresses, their long, elegant fingers plucking only the extreme tips of the tea bushes as they drift down the rows. So it is with whins: do not get too greedy or tempted by flowers deeper within the bushes, but focus only on those few florets which extend beyond the tips of those prickly stems, and move on. Even so, after an hour or so, however careful, the fingertips do end up looking like blood-flecked pincushions

And gorse is one of the wines which transmutes as it ferments; linger a little longer in the spring sunshine and you will detect a more cloying under-scent hidden beneath the freshness of coconut. It is that, rather than the delicate coconut, which tends to dominate the wine itself, making for a rather strong and rather medicinal decoction akin to cough medicine if you are unprepared; here certainly is a wine which benefits from blending. Over the years I have progressively reduced the number of flowers per final gallon of wine and steeped them for a few hours only, rather than soaking for two or three days as I might with more delicately scented flowers. And despite the urgency to pick the blossoms when they emerge – one of the first to flower in the spring – I have, over those same years of experiment, learnt by trial and error that late-picked flowers, picked even as late as July or August, seem to offer a less medicinal flavour. I confess this is one I still haven't got quite right yet; but I shall persevere – and at worst it goes all right with lemonade.

FINGAL'S CAVE

Cathula was playing truant again. The real Cathula had of course (if you believe Nigel Tranter) had been the mistress of Somerled, Lord of the Isles. Her namesake now lay at anchor, nosing gently into the rising swell off Staffa. Now uninhabited, the island has an illustrious history, visited over the years by many luminaries such as Johnson and Boswell, Sir Walter Scott, the poets Keats and Wordsworth, the artist J.W. Turner – and of course Mendelssohn. Rumour has it that the island's last private owner, Jock Elliott Junior of New York, had bought it as a wedding present for his wife; what is certain is that to commemorate his wife's 60th birthday he later gifted it to the National Trust for Scotland. With its striking hexagonal basalt columns and deep sea-caverns it is rightly considered by many the eighth wonder of the world.

Harbour seals bobbed around us in the rolling seas as fulmars and kittiwakes flew busily overhead, ferrying food back to young on narrow ledges on the sheer cliffs; and puffins buzzed to and from burrows on the flat turf summit. With their habit of sitting upright in the water and their snub, almost cat-like faces, I have always had a fondness for common seals (to give them their other name). Even when breeding in the early summer, they tend to form smaller colonies than their larger cousins, the grey seal, more like casual aggregations at regular intertidal haul-outs than the true colonies of the harem-breeding grey seal. Unlike grey seals, common seals mate in the water, but mothers do give birth on land at these traditional haul-out sites; the pups can swim and dive at only a few hours old, and mothers and pups move quickly into the water when disturbed. However, during the first few weeks of life, mothers and especially pups do spend a good deal of time hauled out on sandbanks or rocky ledges in caves: the eerie calls of the pups echoing from some hidden haul-out, or cave, sounds almost human and it is no wonder that rumours abounded with early seafarers about sirens or mermaids – or selkies.

Indeed, it is no coincidence that legends of selkies are most common in Scottish, Irish and Faroese folklore; some 80 per cent of the UK's entire population of common seals occurs in these waters. Selkies are said to live as seals in the sea, but shed their skin to become human on land. Male selkies are typically described as being very handsome in their human form and having great seductive powers over human women, whom they may abduct and take to live with them beneath the sea. Female selkies are also exceptionally beautiful in human form, and if a man steals a female selkie's skin while she is ashore in human form she is in his power and is forced to become his wife. Female selkies are said to make excellent wives, but because their true home is the sea they will often be seen gazing at it longingly, and if a female finds her skin she will immediately return to her true home, and to her selkie husband in the sea.

I confess I have since childhood had a continuing fascination with selkies and always wanted to meet one – even though my logical brain assures me the legends arise simply from the short, snub faces, the liquid, forward-pointing eyes, the almost human calls of the common seal and their habit of bobbing upright in the water, just simply watching. In contrast I had no such childhood wish to meet a kelpie.[24]

Populations of both grey and common seals were decimated during outbreaks of distemper virus (related to the distemper virus which affects domestic dogs) in the late 1980s and in 2002 – it is estimated that the outbreak of 1988 killed over 17,000 common seals from a total population of perhaps 50,000 to 60,000 individuals. Before the epidemic both grey seals and common seals were regarded by many as serious pests of marine fisheries and coastal aquaculture – and on

---

24 a mythical Scottish water-horse

various occasions in the past, substantial numbers were culled at regular haul-out sites or breeding beaches in an attempt to reduce population numbers. The cull was largely of pups of the current season, since these cannot take to the water as readily as adults and thus escape; wildlife managers will, however, uneasily acknowledge that even heavy culling of younger animals rarely achieves any significant reduction in total population size of any animal species, since rates of natural mortality are anyway extremely high amongst juveniles – and thus only a small proportion would ultimately have been recruited to the adult population in any event. In retrospect it seems that culling programmes were unlikely ever to have resulted in any lasting reduction in overall population number in the long term. Since the 1970s both species of seals have been protected in the UK, although fishermen may apply for a special licence to shoot seals seen in the vicinity of fishing gear, and there is also undoubtedly some illegal culling due to the perceived competition with fisheries for commercially valuable fish species.

In fact this perception, too, is probably incorrect. What is the more alarming about the culls sanctioned in the past is that recent research suggests they may not have been justified in any case. Population biologists may point out that the culling carried out was destined in any event to have little impact on long-term population sizes; moralists might argue that the only reason that seals were perceived to be in conflict with humanity in the first place was as the direct result of our own past overexploitation of marine fish stocks, forcing men and seals into competition for the dwindling stocks that remain. But still more fundamentally than that, it appears that original case for the prosecution may itself have been flawed, and the seals wrongfully indicted.

Grey seals and common seals were widely believed to cause damage to commercial fisheries in three major ways. Both were believed to compete with humans for stocks of commercial fish, both cause direct damage – to fish stocks and to gear – at netting stations and fish-rearing cages; finally, seals are host to nematode parasites such as codworm which also infest fish and reduce their commercial value. Recent research suggests that in practice there is no evidence for real conflict on two counts of the three.

Although an individual seal which forages close to shore may get a taste for farmed salmon and cause serious problems to stocks of fish and the netting of fish cages in local areas, for the most part both grey and common seals feed as much as 50 miles out to sea. Early work on the diet of both species – based on the analysis of stomach content of seals taken near fishing nets – revealed salmon, trout and white fish as important items; such sampling was however inevitably biased, in that the animals were taken in the immediate vicinity of fishing nets, and stomach contents merely give information on the most recent meal. More recent analyses of faecal material collected from haul-outs throughout the year suggest that by contrast, commercial fish species constitute only a tiny proportion of the seals' diet and that the bulk of their food is comprised of sand eels or other species not important commercially.

The impact of predation by the entire population of grey seals and common seals around our coasts on a significant food species such as the cod was estimated in the late 1980s at less than 3 per cent of the numbers taken by commercial enterprise; numbers of whiting, haddock, plaice or Norway pout taken by seals averaged less than 1 per cent of commercial catches.

The codworm problem is a more complicated one. Both grey seals and common seals are the end-hosts for a number of nematode parasites which must pass an earlier stage of their life cycle in an intermediate host: fish such as cod or herring. The most significant of these parasites in terms of commercial damage is the codworm – and the most important of the two seal species as host to codworm is the grey seal.[25] Levels of codworm in fish from UK waters rose steadily during the 1950s and 1960s, at the same time as the grey seal population was increasing; the connection seems obvious. But obvious is not the same as straightforward, and the life cycle of the parasite is a complicated one. The seal is its final host – host to the reproductive, adult phase: and as in many species of parasitic worms, even one adult in the gut of the final host can shed many hundreds of thousands of fertile eggs. The number of infective larvae that find their way into the intermediate

---

25 Common seals in general carry lighter worm burdens overall, and these tend to be dominated by herring worm.

host is therefore to some extent independent of the numbers of adult worms – and, indeed, of the number of seals. So, reducing the number of seals is unlikely to result in an equivalent reduction in levels of infestation in the fish. In Canadian waters, as in Britain, there has been a recent dramatic increase in codworm infestation – again apparently accompanying a parallel increase in numbers of grey seals; but recent culls there to reduce grey seal populations were not rewarded by any measurable reduction in levels of codworm infestation in fish.

Perhaps the only issue over which there appears little dispute is that both grey seals and common seals can cause significant damage at nets and fish cages. At netting stations they may remove fish completely from the nets, or damage the fish or damage the nets themselves, resulting in substantial costs for repair – and potentially facilitating the escape of any other fish already within the net. Most of these problems occur around static gear, particularly nets set for salmon and tangle nets. Damage, in this case particularly by common seals, may also occur at fish cages moored offshore for the rearing of farmed fish; seals are regarded as the most serious source of loss at salmon farms, but even here it appears that the issues relate in the main to a few problem individuals who have adjusted to these easy pickings, just as predation on lambs by hill foxes is also commonly a habit acquired by only certain individual foxes.

∗∗∗

While I mused about seals and selkies, Ewan had hauled on the bow rope to bring *Cathula*'s tender alongside: a snub-nosed rib.[26] He hinged open the guard rail, and Cathy and I dropped overboard into the rib. Ewan joined us, and surrounded by the skimming puffins we headed out towards the huge opening of Fingal's Cave. From sea level the towering black columns of basalt were impressive in their almost perfect hexagonal section – supporting, as if in some geological facsimile of an Athenian temple, the amorphous volcanic tuff of the island's 'capstone'.

This image of some gigantic ancient acropolis was enhanced by the scattering of broken columns littering the shallow water, which

---

26 rigid inflatable boat

looked for all the world like the fallen columns I had seen in the temple of Athene broken into their component cog-wheel cylinders as they fell (albeit those had been sandy in colour and with a ribbed circumference). It always seems remarkable to me that these same basalt columns can be seen on Eigg – and that the columns of Staffa continue under the sea until they emerge again, many miles away, as the Giant's Causeway in County Antrim.

The mouth of the cave loomed huge and black. The tide was on the turn towards the ebb, and it was Ewan's fancy to use the power of the rib's outboard to rush in on an incoming wave to the furthest recesses of the cave and then turn, to surf out again as that wave receded, using the rib, I suppose, as a kind of power-assisted surfboard. Possibly somewhat unorthodox, probably totally against any health and safety protocol, but a jolly escapade all the same.

He timed it to perfection: in we barrelled on the rolling wave to the back of the cave – at low tide one can of course walk at least part of the way on a safety-railed ledge of rock, but that isn't half as much fun. At the very last moment, he kicked the outboard into reverse, spun the rib, and out we surfed. Somehow, despite the evocative images of Turner's paintings, or Mendelssohn's 'Hebrides Overture', I don't believe they can have had quite the same thrill. Then as the light began to fail, we puttered back amongst the black wreckage of the fallen columns and the bobbing seals to scramble back aboard *Cathula* and make the long journey back to Lethinnis.

SHAKESPEARE IN THE BIG HOUSE

Despite a reputed irascibility, the Laird had a genuine affection for his staff and the wider community; he had after all been visiting Lochuisge and The Aunt since he was himself a young man. While he and his wife did not always participate in person in the goings-on of the village or the hall, they never-failingly provided a raffle prize of a hamper, or a (butchered) lamb carcass from the Estate for the Christmas Draw. The fine old Big House, also, while showing its age and the shabby elegance of a decaying gentility, was a superb stage set for productions by The Players.

In past eras the gentry of the area had been the Laird, the Minister and the Dominie (head teacher) – those, in effect, whom probably birth, and certainly education, had separated out from the farm labourers and crofters of the general populace over the years. But now, as Lochuisge and the neighbouring villages began to absorb their share of incomers, and more and more of both native and immigrant population were more cultured and more widely read, that historic educational divide was collapsing.

They also had more leisure time, since in a more prosperous society the requirements of simply earning even a subsistence living were relaxed. And while Lochuisge and Camas Inas did not have the population (or perhaps the interest) to produce an amateur dramatic group, enough people within the wider peninsula now had the enthusiasm and ambition to mount an annual production.

One I particularly recall was a performance of *Twelfth Night* enacted by wandering, scene by scene, amongst the libraries, drawing rooms and great entrance hall of the Big House, accompanied by the gentle music of the clarsach and the Jester's fiddle – an unfolding drama followed by an audience as keen to gawp at the draperies of the ballroom or drawing room as to follow the intricacies of Shakespeare's comedy. Some of the subtlety of the play (if *Twelfth Night* is ever subtle) and of the resounding, reverberating poetry was perhaps somewhat lost in the nervousness of a shy and naturally soft-spoken Orsino (a peaceable and rather reserved hill-shepherd from the Saimhairidh Estate), whom discomfort at such public performance reduced to an almost inaudible whisper. But the oddly-cast Mairi, as a female Belch, was a comedic triumph – and the local doctor's Malvolio put quite another complexion on his character for those timetabled to attend the surgery the following day.

And so through the labyrinth of the Big House we wandered, like strolling players ourselves, to admire the simulated shipwreck on the front lawn or peer at the exquisite hand-painted friezes of flowers and fruits in the ballroom – relics of The Aunt's occupation – while straining to catch the whispered tones of Orsino (whose attractive partner in real life portrayed a very convincing and rather forceful Olivia).

'Come away, come away, death. And in sad cypress let me be laid … I am slain by a fair cruel maid.' The strains of Feste's fiddle echoed through the panelled halls as the equally labyrinthine plot of Shakespeare's play unravelled towards the triumphant climax when all is revealed and all live happily ever after: 'When that I was, and a little tiny boy (with hey, ho, the wind and the rain).'

SHIPWRECKS AND
THE LITTLE PRINCESS

There was a shuddering, wrenching crash, startling the dogs and rattling the window sashes – ill-fitting at the best of times – within their frames. This was no summer storm, for the night was calm, if somewhat overcast, with the usual grey rollers in the bay. Possibly a tree down, because after weeks of rain the ground was pretty well waterlogged. Even large trees were comparatively shallow-rooted in the thin soil; compensating for the fact that because of the underlying rock their roots could not penetrate far below the surface, they grew wide root plates over a significant area; in such waterlogged conditions, turning the sparse earth to mud, they were prone simply to uproot themselves and topple. Down at the Mains, John Petherick got up and took a tour around the house and stable yard to check for damage as far as he was able by the limited light of an old torch. He could see little of import and went back into the kitchen to brew up the first cup of tea of the morning. He took a cup through to Judy and settled at the table with his habitual matchstick-thin roll-up and the crossword.

It was only when the day gradually lightened and Judy emerged into the kitchen that she noticed that the – presumably timeless – view from the window of the Mains had been altered by the addition, centre-stage, of the huge prow of an enormous tanker ploughed ashore on the rocky beach below. Still more bizarrely, instead of a scurrying army of personnel swarming all over the vessel, it appeared to be completely abandoned.

Larger shipping was supposed to avoid the Inner Minch and take the outer route between the Inner Hebrides and the Outer Isles, but commonly to save time and fuel would take a shortcut through the inner channel. In this case the Lithuanian crew of the *Gullfoss* had failed to make the turn in time and driven her straight onto the rocks. Indeed there was no evidence they had tried to turn at all – the ship looked as if she had pursued a dead-straight course past the tip of Mull; rumour spread quickly that in fact at the time of the accident no one had been on the bridge, but all had been below decks watching television. We were lucky, I guess that she was not breached, for the *Gullfoss* was a large oil tanker; by good fortune – and perhaps because she had driven straight up the shore – she was not holed, but simply well aground with the huge ploughshare shoe at the base of the keel well embedded in the rocks well above the current tideline. It was equally clear, however, that she could not be floated off or even hauled off by tugs until the next really high tide, and that she was to become a feature of the landscape for some weeks to come.

This, sadly, was no latter-day SS *Politician* and *Whisky Galore*. The concern remained that while the tanker was not holed at present, relentless grinding against the rocks as she rolled to and fro in the half-tides might in time wear through the steel plates of the hull and rupture some on the internal tanks before the tide was high enough to refloat her. The coastguard busied themselves positioning inflatable booms around the tanker and across the mouth of the bay.

This was by no means the first – or would be the last – such shipping disaster in the Sound. Nor indeed was it the first time a skipper might have been less than alert at the wheel: there was a skipper in Lochbuidhe never known by his given name but always referred to as the Sleepy Captain after a similar grounding of a passenger ferry 40 years before. The Sound was in fact a litter of wrecks, some recent, many ancient, which now served as hiding places or artificial reefs for lobsters and langoustines and lurking marine eels – those same wrecks made the area as popular with the local lobster fishermen as with the many (human) divers who visited the area explicitly to dive amongst the wrecks, some simply for pleasure, others with a more academic interest in marine archaeology. Amongst the wrecks are a number of ships from the period of the Jacobite rebellion, sent by the English to bombard the Catholic coastline of Lethinnis, as well as reports of others dating from much earlier: vessels reputedly sunk while fleeing the defeat of the Spanish Armada in 1588.

Local legend claims the Armada fleet had been accompanied by a beautiful Spanish princess who had been visited in a dream by a vision of the man she must marry. When the famous *Florencia* arrived in Tobermory on Mull, the princess, sailing on that ship, found the man of her dream to be Sir Lachlan Maclean of Duart. She made no secret of her pilgrimage to find him, and word soon reached the ears of Sir Lachlan's wife; she instructed a manservant to board the ship and drop a slow-burning fuse into the powder magazine of the *Florencia* before making his own escape. The resulting explosion destroyed the entire vessel and all those on board including the little princess. A different tradition reports that the *Florencia* had put into Tobermory to buy provisions, and that the ship was fired following a dispute over payment, sinking the vessel and an immense fortune of gold bullion; but that ship may not have been the *Florencia*, but another ship of the retreating Armada fleet, the *San Juan de Sicilia* (or *San Juan de Baptista*), which carried troops, not treasure. Whatever the true story, no significant treasure has ever been recovered in Tobermory Bay – but in St Columba's Church in Kinlochbuidhe there is a tomb attributed to Princess Clara Viola.

Lochuisge Mains itself had been conceived (once more by the Gordons, former lairds of Lochuisge) as a 'model' farmstead – built in the late 19th century as an exemplar of what a modern farm might be, with a delightful two-storey house set in one side of an enclosed courtyard of substantial stone-built outbuildings. Many of these retained the original fittings and features – the old partitioned stalls of the byre and stable, the high vaulted roofs of the barn and hay store.

It was actually a beautiful set-up in a beautiful spot, but the current Laird had not the funds to maintain them, and both they and the house itself were falling into some disrepair. Swallows flitted in and out of the broken arrow-slit windows of the byres. The house was damp and difficult to heat: as with Allt na Mhuillin, ill-fitting windows meant that any heat generated was contributing more to heating a wider Scotland than the world within, our personal contributions to global warming being more direct than simply through emission of greenhouse gases. The access track, too, was a nightmare: a steep and twisting, rutted track which tore the suspension from a succession of battered vehicles despite John's mechanical and welding skills. But despite the difficulties, John and Judy contrived to make the place cheerful and welcoming; chickens scratched in the yard, geese in the old orchard and the three ponies always cantered over quickly to welcome any visitors.

Besides the croft, John worked as a blacksmith. That perhaps is overstating it, because it presumes he ever did much work. He was in fact an extremely skilled metalworker, but equally skilled at putting off the evil moment when he might have to get out of his chair and lock himself in his smithy; there was more than a grain of truth in his half-joke against himself in response to a complaint from a customer about endless delays: 'Well I did indeed promise it to you for Christmas, but I didn't say which Christmas!' He was a smith rather than a farrier, and while his bread and butter (such as it was) was derived from fixing up old and battered farm machinery or repairing gates and railings, his actual pleasure in the smithy was in turning out fine ornamental work. It was always something of a surprise to see these fine and delicate pieces of his own design emerging under those huge, gnarled hands and fingers: ramshead companion sets for the fireside; gleaming, finely polished paper knives perhaps surmounted by a rearing stallion – or, as a gift to us, a perfectly wrought goat's head. But even in making such exquisite items he never over-exerted himself – a genuine pity, because he and Judy were in a constant battle financially and he could indeed have made a very good living at this fine work had he applied himself: demand was always significantly greater than supply. But there was always a reason to be doing something else; to his credit, the policies around the Mains were always immaculately maintained with well-made and well-hung fences and gates; unlike almost every other gate on the peninsula, you never had to lift one of John's gates into place – it swung sweetly back to latch itself closed.

And besides his talents with metal, John himself was an enthusiastic and talented cook. Relatively self-sufficient like ourselves, he always had home-grown meat in the freezer and home-grown vegetables in the rack. The only problem in accepting an invitation to dinner (apart from the damage inflicted by the access track on any vehicle) was that John would rarely start to prepare before your arrival. Indeed, if you had been invited for eight o'clock, it was quite likely that the Rayburn would not even be lit when you arrived (the courteous ten minutes late). By the time that was lit and up to temperature, the meat was in, vegetables were prepared and added to the roasting tray, it might be one o'clock in the morning before the meal was ready to be served. By this time, however delicious might be the food that John laid out on the table, you were often past eating, with the ravenous appetite with which you had perhaps had arrived completely disappeared some hours before – or assuaged in the meantime, whiling away the wait, with copious quantities of cheap wine, so that you were simply too tipsy or sleepy to be able to face food. Getting home to Allt na Mhuillin along the steep track and through the various Estate gates was in itself an additional challenge.

THE WHITE COCKADE

Catholic Lethinnis had certainly featured centre-stage in the Jacobite uprising of 1745.

Bonnie Prince Charlie had led the insurrection, not – as many might imagine – for his own immediate restoration as monarch but on behalf of his father, James Edward Stuart, son of the deposed King James II (as many a prince did go to war in their father's name). The timing had been fortuitous; because most of the British Army was on the European continent, fighting in the larger War of the Austrian Succession, comparatively few troops were left in England to respond to the unexpected coup from the north.

So near and yet so far: Charles landed on the isle of Eriskay on 23 July 1745 and, with word quickly spread to loyal clansmen, assembled a force, raised his standard at Glenfinnan on 19 August, and marched his men southwards, then across the border into England. One might wonder why after its early successes in Scotland, the Jacobite army essayed further south at all – after all, Scotland was in its hands and the English there had been soundly defeated. In fact, despite the army's early successes, the bulk of Charles Edward Stuart's more seasoned advisers had advised against pursuing the campaign too far to the south, arguing vehemently for a retreat north of the border to consolidate their position, eliminate government forces still in the north and wait for the promised French assistance. Part of the advisers' concern was also rooted in the fear that the various volunteer or conscripted clansmen might start to feel they had been away from home and croft for too long and thus begin to drift away in their ones and twos to return and attend to hearth and harvests, diminishing the Jacobite force.

But Charles and his supporters believed that their army was made for moving, and believed that they had the advantage of both surprise and their early success: the bonnie prince was here to win back the British throne and believed that his best chance was to strike south before too many forces could be recalled from France. In addition, while people often think of the Jacobite rebellions as a purely Scottish affair, the uprising was in fact strongly supported (in word if not in deed) by a number of English Tory Jacobites keen to re-establish a Stuart on the British throne. Knowing this, Charles was sure that if his army pressed on they would receive reinforcement on their triumphant way south.

The Jacobites took Carlisle and reached Derby on 4 December. A council meeting was convened the following day. Again the bonnie prince's senior advisers (the Lords Elcho, Ogilvy and Murray) began by arguing for a retreat to Scotland. They knew of at least two British armies in England. One, led by Augustus, Duke of Cumberland, the son of George I, Elector of Hanover, lay to the south between them and their target of London. The other army, led by General Wade (he who, to facilitate future rapid movements of English troops, subsequently designed and engineered many of the military roads and bridges that still persist throughout the Highland region), was to the north of their current position. Wade had in fact led a force from Newcastle to Carlisle on 16 November, by which time Carlisle had already fallen to the Jacobites.

Then, as is the stuff of intrigue (you couldn't make this up) a certain Dudley Bradstreet – who was in fact an English spy – informed Charles of new intelligence: there was a third army, returned from France under the command of either Lieutenant General Hawley or Lieutenant General Ligonier, with 9,000 soldiers, who also now stood between Charles' army and London. This information – as it turns out, a complete fabrication – tipped the balance, and Charles reluctantly agreed to retreat to Scotland, with in theory only General Wade's forces in his army's path. It has all the ingredients of a much more modern tale. The retreating Jacobite army engaged in a skirmish with British forces at Clifton, Cumbria, on 18 December and subsequently lost control of Carlisle in a siege, lasting from 21 December to the 30th. Early the following year the Jacobites were defeated at the Battle of Littleferry, and on 16 April suffered their final defeat, and near-annihilation, at Culloden: amongst the fallen, the Jacobite clansmen of Charles Maclean of Lochuisge.

Reprisals were swift and brutal. English warships in the Sound bombarded the Lethinnis coast from the sea, and the peninsula was put to the torch; stone cannonballs littered the coastline, and as we dug the walled vegetable gardens of Allt na Mhuillin we frequently unearthed more.

The whole episode has become somewhat romanticised and overlaid with subsequent, largely Victorian mawkishness, with tales of Flora MacDonald and 'Speed Bonny Boat'. But the true historical facts are stark enough; the Scottish army, even without the promised assistance from France and the never-forthcoming assistance from English sympathisers, had proved an extremely effective force – and history might have been very different but for the false information relayed by Dudley Bradstreet. Even in the tale of Flora MacDonald and the prince's escape, there was an underlying memory of the truth: Flora MacDonald, daughter of Ranald MacDonald of Milton, was living on the island of Benbecula in the Outer Hebrides when Bonnie Prince Charlie took refuge there after the Battle of Culloden. Captain Conn O'Neill, the prince's companion, sought her assistance to help the prince escape capture; after some hesitation, Flora promised to do so. The island was controlled by the Hanoverian government using a local militia, and in another bizarre twist of fate (you really couldn't make this stuff up), the commander of that militia force was her stepfather, Hugh MacDonald. He gave her a pass to the mainland for herself, a manservant, an Irish spinning maid, Betty Burke, and a boat's crew of six men. Charles Edward Stuart, with a price on his head of £30,000, was disguised as Betty Burke, and the escape was successful.

For a while almost the very idea of Scottishness was banned, along with the wearing of the tartan and the playing of the pipes, and the lands of those who had supported the uprising, for the most part forfeited. But many of these properties were subsequently restored, and by 1815 the Jacobite cause was no longer seen a political threat. At Glenfinnan, Alexander Macdonald, 10th Laird of Glenaladale, commissioned a fine monument to commemorate the raising of the standard there some 70 years earlier. While this fine monument at the head of Loch Shiel is well known (and must feature in more photographs of the Highlands than any other artefact, with perhaps the sole exception of the castle at Eilean Donan), what is perhaps less well known is that it was never paid for. Alexander lived a life of extravagant show and died the following year at the age of just 28, having squandered the family fortunes. The architect of the famous monument, James Gillespie Graham, was among the creditors at his death.

Two other facets of the affair often escape the tourist. First, old lithographs make it clear that the tower itself was originally attached to a long two-storey building to one side, used as a gun room or shooting box; this was later removed by Angus Macdonald, the son of the original patron of the monument; subsequent to the removal of this effective buttress, the tower has started to lean. At the same time, young Angus added the octagonal perimeter wall and the statue of the Highland chieftain at the top of the tower itself. That crowning statue, carved by stonemason John Greenshields, is also something of an enigma. Many people believe it is supposed to be an image of the bonnie prince himself, but the story is told that the sculptor was directed to a portrait of the prince in the collection of a noble house in Perthshire to make the sketches. At the time of his visit the owners were not at home and he was shown into the first-floor gallery by a housemaid who did not know which of the many canvasses on display portrayed the prince himself; so, selecting the only one with tartan trews as a likely candidate, the sculptor in fact carved what is now at least dignified as a portrait of the 'Unknown Highlander'.

The Unknown Highlander stares out over Loch Shiel, turning his back on the viaduct over which still thunders the Jacobite steam train to Mallaig, and Harry Potter's Hogwarts Express.

FIRE DOWN BELOW

Many communities in this part of the Highlands, of necessity, maintained their own volunteer or more formal fire crews. Angy was a retained firefighter in the retained Fire Service in An Drochaid, one of the villages across on the mainland. This nice distinction of 'retained', as opposed to 'volunteer', service simply meant that for our part-time support we received a small, but regular, pay cheque from the Highlands and Islands Fire Service; if called out to a fire we also received a small bonus – a bonus which was greatly increased if that fire happened to be at night or over the weekend. Alongside his work as a firefighter, Angy, like many others, had a second job; he worked for the council, too, and had the use of a council van.

That season there had been an unusual spate of hill fires, often at weekends, and more than it seemed were likely to have been started simply by careless cigarettes flicked from the window of a passing car. Local rumour began to spread that some bright spark in the An Drochaid crew had cottoned on to a possible money-spinner in that if they could be sure of a small hill fire on a Sunday, and sure that they would then be called out to extinguish it, this could sustain a more reliable injection of overtime rates to the take-home pay at the end of the month. Suspicions grew as more and more of these weekend fires seemed to be starting at the roadside; more than once a council van had been spotted parked in the vicinity before the fire spread. In the end, as one of these weekend fires raged out of control through a forestry plantation and threatened to engulf An Drochaid itself, the police had to take the rumours more seriously. Angy's van was pulled in, and it turned out that the on-board tracking device installed by the council had recorded the vehicle as being in the vicinity of each recent fire half an hour before each one had been reported. What amazed us – and the Sheriff Court, subsequently – was that the man had not thought to disable the tracker or to use a vehicle other than his council van for his illegal fire-raising.

Because of our geography – Lethinnis, more than most, being a comparatively self-reliant community – we too boasted our own retained fire brigade on the basis that if there was a fire on the peninsula it could take an hour or more for a fire engine to attend from the mainland, across the Narrows, by which time it would likely be too late to do anything but warm one's hands and roast potatoes in the embers. The fire station (a somewhat glorified title for the converted garage in which the shiny red fire engine was parked) was in Kinlochbuidhe. Despite a constant shortage of recruits there was some hesitation about accepting my application: rivalries between Kinlochbuidhe and Lochuisge persisted – and in any case, if I were called to a fire, it might take me 20 minutes to join the rest of the crew. In vain, I protested that others too, might take as long as that to reach the fire station even if they lived and worked closer, because they would have to leave their work, perhaps come in from distant fields if they were employed as shepherds or stockmen – and that if the fire was by chance between Lochuisge and Kinlochbuidhe, I could meet the rest of the crew at the fire itself. Not that we had many. In the event (and I am sure that it was in sheer desperation to get the crew up to minimum required strength or lose the facility altogether) my application was accepted.

For the record I was never the last to arrive at the station or last to a fire – not that we had many to attend. As we were a retained force however, it was all taken comparatively seriously and we had regular practices every fortnight when we would take the machine from its shed, practise rolling and unrolling the long canvas hoses, check the pumps – we carried a significant volume of water in tanks within the vehicle itself which made it a pig to drive, but also had suction pumps so that we could where necessary avail ourselves of water from nearby burns or pools, or even more rarely some occasional unexpected fire hydrant. Beset by midges much of the time, since they also frequent the deeper pools beneath the trees which we would exploit for a water supply, we would rehearse potential (if unlikely) scenarios, and practise ladder work and the use of the high-pressure steel nozzles or 'branches'.

Actually, it had its serious side and although good-natured we all realised that if the worst came to the worst we were the front line in any emergency. But for the most part – and certainly in practice – we were employed more for using our ladders and water jets to clean people's gutters or hose down the outside of Kinlochbuidhe Hall than in fighting fires.

We were a fully politically-correct force of all ages and both sexes: Lindsay and her daughter Eilidh from the shop; Kay, who worked as a receptionist at the primary school – a bubbly, giggly woman full of mischief who could put us all in stitches but who could pull her weight in a crisis; Rob-the-Bus; two or three of the local shepherds; and Dougie from the quarry. This motley crew were kept in some semblance of order by Iain as senior fire officer who worked otherwise in the roads department of the council, maintaining the tarmac of the single-tracked road back out to the ferry at Caol, and clearing any blocked culverts or overgrown ditches. In winter he switched to the snowplough, and it was he who went out at all hours to clear and grit the road over that same high pass to Caol before venturing further afield within the peninsula. In consequence he knew everyone and everywhere, every back road and unmade track leading to the most remote croft.

Part of our regular training was to learn these same byways and also visit the larger (and potentially more vulnerable) houses in the area to check out their internal layout, the location of doors and staircases – and the nearest water supply. While the fire crew had regularly been round the mansion houses of Ardslignish and Saimhairidh, they had in the past never explored the Big House at Lochuisge – or Allt na Mhuillin. I think the latter trip was more of an excuse for a cup of tea than anything else, but I well remember Iain's surprise that while we maintained our own private water supply to the house from a spring high up the hillside, we did also have a mains supply only a few yards away along the track and boasted our own fire hydrant. Fires were in truth few and far between – and for the most part simply chimney fires when someone had omitted to close down the draught sufficiently and the fire had caught the accumulated soot and creosote layering the chimney from the burning of improperly seasoned firewood. But even those were serious enough, and we had to take real care to make sure the scorching heat within the chimney had not caused some spontaneous ignition of wooden beams butted into that same overheated stonework. But these were all our neighbours, and as like as not, while we waited to make sure the fire was truly quelled – and helped to clear up any mess we had occasioned in the meantime – there was always time for another cup of tea or perhaps a dram (for all but Iain, who was the driver).

Sadly, this relaxed approach to an essential community service changed all too quickly with the advent of all the new rules and regulations designed to protect our health and safety – and protect, no doubt, our employers from responsibility or, worse still, some injury claim. Regular practices came to be supervised by a more senior official brought in each week from Invergordon or Inverness. New rules sprung up about ladder work, about who could actually enter a burning building. The minimally staffed crew was declared not big enough to qualify for training in the modern breathing apparatus required if we were to be allowed into smoke-filled buildings ...

It all became a bit of a nightmare and while we struggled to retain our easy camaraderie, it became less of a different form of relaxation and more of a proper job. Yet how could we accept the restrictions? These were our neighbours and friends; how could we not enter a building simply because we did not have the appropriate breathing apparatus when a burning house might not be empty but somewhere within might be an elderly neighbour overcome by smoke and fumes? I never came to accept this over-protection of self-interest: after all, we had all been fully aware when we had signed up that fighting fire is a potentially dangerous occupation – surely a bit self-evident – and were by definition prepared to accept calculated risk.

My last call-out before compulsory retirement at 55 came with a phone call from the central HQ at two in the morning: a vehicle on fire in the car park of the Social Club in Kinlochbuidhe; few further details were offered except for the fact that the vehicle appeared to have been abandoned. I threw the magnetic flasher on top of the pickup and flew down the road. As Dougie and I met at the fire station and pulled on our uniforms,[27] it emerged we were the only two who had responded to the call. We pulled back the heavy doors and I took the big vehicle out into the night. Dougie stepped quickly onto the running board and we headed the few hundred yards down to the club – the same club where Donnie and I had often shared a post-fishing beer, so it was easy enough to find and, with the car ablaze up against the rear wall of the club itself, we needed no searchlights. The only problem was that the blazing car sat astride a number of gas cylinders toppled from the club's store of spent cylinders, stacked up against that same back wall.

Full cylinders usually have enough liquid gas within them that they aren't especially volatile; half-used or spent cylinders by contrast have an almost perfect mix of gas and airspace to make them highly explosive – and these were getting hot. To me, the situation epitomised the conflict of modern over-regulation. With two of us present we were in no way a full crew, and were not in any way obliged to try and tackle a potentially dangerous situation; but if we did not the implications were unimaginable. In truth we ourselves would have no protection from a potential blast – there was no wall behind which we could conceal ourselves while tackling the fire, and any such screen would have been poor protection anyway in the event of an explosion. On the plus side it appeared that – at least at present – only the tyres of the car were on fire and the flames had not, as yet, spread to ignite the petrol tank. Somewhat apprehensively, we foamed the tyres from close range with portable extinguishers, before pulling back to pick up our branches and soak the pile of gas cylinders with a stream of water from high-pressure hoses.

Seeing the lights from the fire engine, Beathag appeared from her house across the road; it was she who had raised the alarm just half an hour before. It appeared that one of her regulars had left the club

---

27 Firefighters' over-trousers are always left rolled down around the outside of the heavy boots so that boots and trousers can be pulled on in a single heave.

sometime after midnight, having had to her certain count at least 12 large whiskies (and Scottish measures are larger than those dispensed south of the border). Getting into his car to drive the half a mile of so through the village to his home, he had in his confusion engaged first gear rather than reverse. and before realising his mistake had rammed the car hard into the side wall of the club. He found reverse, only to discover that the initial impact had locked the front bumper of the vehicle around the stonework on the corner of the building and reverse gear wasn't doing anything at all. In desperation he rammed the accelerator to the floor; the wheels spun on the tarmac and grew so hot that the rubber started to burn. Eventually the trapped bumper wrenched away from the front of the car, which rocketed backwards to hit and dislodge some of the piled gas cylinders, coming to rest against the remainder. Giro (I don't think I ever knew his real name; he was simply known to everyone as Giro in honour of the benefit cheque he received each week from the Unemployment) had considered discretion the better part of valour and had legged it home to bed on foot.

I never did hear the end of the tale and whether or not Giro was prosecuted; he certainly didn't have a car any more, to be done for drunk-driving.

I followed his example and headed home.

A WEDDING AND A FUNERAL

The church sat by itself in a little birch-fringed bay beneath the road, gazing out across Camas a'Choire towards Shuna. Generously endowed by previous lairds at a time when it was good to be seen to be embracing the church, it was light and airy and sported a number of remarkably fine pieces of stained glass in the windows – windows worthy of far greater cathedrals than a simple village church. For much of the time it lazed in comparative peace; there was no resident minister and services were held only every fortnight when the Minister visited from Kinlochbuidhe.

A cat from one of the nearby cottages tended to curl up for sleep in one of the un-stained windows, and two half-tame stags grazed on the foreshore or sheltered in the birches behind the church itself; unlike other deer, which tended to draw out to the open hill beyond over the summer months, these two veterans seemed content to hang around the church all year. Perhaps the constant offshore breezes kept away the midges and other biting insects that their fellows climbed high into the hills to avoid. And no local stalker was going to molest them here.

The regular routine of fortnightly services was disturbed only for high days and holidays and as a general rule weddings and funerals involved the whole community. In an ageing population, weddings were rare, but Seonaid's nephew Brian was wed in Lochuisge and I myself had remarried, more quietly, in the pretty church. In our case, and by our choice, only the Minister, the two witnesses and Cathy's children had been invited to attend, but the cat sunned itself in the window and as we left the church after the simple service, the two resident stags shaded themselves under the trees in the front of the church.

By contrast in this same ageing population funerals were increasingly common. In this part of the Highlands it was still common practice for the coffin to remain at the house for neighbours and well-wishers to pay their respects to the deceased. It was also not uncommon for friends and neighbours to hold a wake to remember, and yet to celebrate the life their friend had led. These were far from solemn occasions, even while the coffin might rest at one end of the same room; indeed, the coffin served usefully as an extra surface on which one might rest a glass. I remember one such wake in Camas Inas. Neillie Macdonald – who had been on Eriskay as a lad at the time of the sinking of the *Politician* – had lived to a good age, and while we missed him and his keen sense of mischief, the wake was indeed more a remembrance of a good life well lived than a mourning of his passing. Indeed, for us, a wake was much like any other party: drink flowed particularly freely, while people stood and chatted animatedly in different clusters within the room and consumed abundant quantities of home-made sandwiches, and young Niall, the tractor driver, sat in another corner quietly playing gentle, if haunting, Gaelic airs on his accordion.

The funeral service itself might once again be held at the house or perhaps a day or two later in the church – now filled again with flowers. The usual service, the usual readings, the eulogies from friends and family. But to the closing strains on organ or keyboard, perhaps of 'Sunset over Sunart', 'The Dark Island', 'Farewell to Fiunary' or the great swirling melody of 'Highland Cathedral', the cortege would leave house or church and wind slowly up to the burial ground high above the village. It seems usual in this part of the Highlands, and I have noted the same in villages on Skye, that the graveyard is often outside and well above the village – and ours had the most spectacular of views, out along the loch and west toward America.

Fortunately in this more modern era, graves were dug by machine and did not need to be excavated by hand. But no hearse could attempt the track or the steepness of the climb through two sheep parks to the burial ground itself, so the coffin was carried on foot by relays of bearers until we reached the graveside. Those who had done their shift, or others awaiting their call in due turn, walked along behind the coffin in small groups strung out along the track, chatting quietly with other neighbours and mourners. Interments were indeed a more solemn occasion than the preceding wake, but on the whole more peaceful than sad – and somehow the humbling vastness of the view, the simple grandeur of the landscape, brought a fitting sense of perspective and proportion.

CORALS, COWRIE SHELLS
AND A SOLAR ECLIPSE

The dogs ran loose around us, casting to and fro among the dunes as we walked down the last bit of the track to the bay. The whippet was beside herself: we had acquired her when she was already two years old and the chief obsession of her earlier life had been chasing rabbits. Lethinnis had no rabbits so she was permanently unfulfilled – but here at Langamull in the north of Mull there were bunnies everywhere and her brain was about to explode. The other dogs were just as aware of the rabbits, but more concerned with reaching the beach ahead.

We picked our way the last few yards through the dense machair onto the soft white sand of the beach and loosed the dogs still on leashes. In those days we had quite a pack: an assortment of pointers, three salukis and a mongrel terrier as well as the besotted whippet, and they all loved walks along the beach. As always, we had the beach to ourselves so were not too concerned about disturbing others in the first few minutes of frenzied barking as the dogs hared to and fro along the firm sand at the water's edges, occasionally breaking off to dash into the sea and splash among the last breath of the dying waves as they finally foundered on the shore. Turnstones and knots foraged the same shore line behind the receding tide, not greatly put off by the blundering dogs.

This part of Mull offered little bays where rocky promontories protected curving beaches of brilliant white sand. As on many beaches, the sand is essentially made of the powdered shells of sea creatures –

and there is a preponderance in these parts of cockles and top shells, giving it a predominantly white colour; but in fact on these beaches in the north of Mull, as elsewhere in the islands, much of the sand was actually composed of fragmented coral. In my childhood imaginings of the world, corals – and cowries come to that – were something associated with remote tropical beaches; I had no conception that they both could be found in UK waters, although admittedly the corals were probably less colourful than some of their tropical cousins. And while the dogs dashed about on the firmer sand left by the falling tide, we walk along the strandline higher up the beach looking for larger pieces of coral or the pretty pink cowrie shells and any other interesting or decorative jetsam like the fragile and translucent cast shells of shore crabs or particularly colourful fragments of mussel shell or sea urchin tests. The cowries, I would later make into pendants or other jewellery, just for the pleasure, not for any commercial market; the rest we would keep, and indeed our bathroom accumulates an ever-growing collection of such treasures.

Perhaps because they faced a long sea loch, rather than the open sea, the rockier beaches of Lethinnis rarely accumulated much to interest the beachcomber, although we usually returned home from any excursion with perhaps a useful length of rope or some fish-boxes, or some salt-soaked baulk of timber which could be put to good building use once soaked free of its salt. As a result, we enjoyed the contrast of these rare outings to a more open coastline just as much as the dogs did. Besides Langamull, another favourite was the silver sand of the beaches by Arisaig, looking out over the wide seas towards the sharp peaked silhouette of Rum and the surprising Sgurr of Eigg. These beaches too had cowries and corals (and to the whippet's great delight, more rabbits); the children could plunge-dive like gannets from the rockier outcrops. On sunnier days we could later picnic on the sand, lighting a fire with driftwood to barbecue sausages and burgers (and marshmallows) or whatever we might have brought with us. We usually took plastic plates, but for cutlery we would set to, to collect a matching set of razor shells to use as knives, and equally carefully selected lantern shells for spoons and forks. However charred on the outside and raw on the inside, such impromptu meals with their improvised utensils were always tastier than those conventionally cooked indoors. And if push came to shove, there was always the option of stovies or cullen skink in one of the cafes in Mallaig.

I loved the many varied colours of these beaches: the sandy-yellow beaches of the far north (where cowries are called groatie buckies), the bright-white beaches of the western coasts of the mainland and the Hebridean islands, the rippled silver-grey mud of Inverie on Knoydart and the stunning red sands of Applecross – as many different colours as those of Alum Bay in the Isle of Wight, 600 miles to the south, but simply spread over a wider compass. I loved, too, the myriad of birds along the shore or in the shallow waters beyond: the glorious eiders crooning quietly in the tidal shallows off Applecross; the turnstones, knots and ringed plovers of Arisaig and the noisy, boisterous Arctic terns bickering above the small burn of fresh water crossing the exposed tidal sand.

Here at Langamull, tired now of rampaging along the beach and barking at the waves, the dogs had turned to fossicking in the tumbled seaweed of the strandline or ducking their heads into rock pools at the edge of the bay, looking for something dead to roll in or better still to eat. Rhoda, one of the older pointers, liked a well-ripened dead fish almost as much as peacock poo, and while small children might associate a day at the seaside with ice cream or candyfloss the highlight of Rhoda's outing was scavenging for mussels or cockles, or even small crabs left stranded by the tide, to sick them up again with enthusiasm in the car on the journey home. The whippet was morose now that there were no rabbits to chase – and all that Fliss required was for someone to throw something for her to retrieve. Endlessly. We always got tired of the game long before she did. Sticks were much requested but risky (we had once suffered the veterinary costs of a punctured pharynx, when she had leapt to catch a stick end-on and then stumbled, ramming the sharp end through her soft palate); stones hurled into the sea, while pursued among the waves with enthusiasm, tended to sink, to her total bemusement. Fortunately some previous visitor had left behind a soggy green tennis ball; she wasn't the softest-mouthed retriever of all time, so it wouldn't survive for long, but it might last the distance.

Although well-bred and from working stock, Fliss was never going to become a working pointer; built more in the shape of a male than affecting the slimmer lines of a bitch, she was clumsy – and gun-shy, which didn't help. We had discovered this while she was a puppy, having mistakenly taken this rather flashy German Shorthaired pointer with us on our annual outing to the Highland Game Fair; all was going well and friends and colleagues were all admiring the classy puppy. Cathy had drawn ahead while I lingered outside one of the many stalls to talk to a current colleague: stalker on one of the big Estates where I was presently working (the Fair was always a good opportunity to catch up with such colleagues on an informal basis – over the years I don't think I have ever got completely round the showground). At the edge of my hearing I caught someone calling my name and from the far corner of my eye saw Cathy being dragged precipitately in the opposite direction, tripping over guy-ropes of marquees and other obstacles in apparently headlong flight. I hurried in pursuit: my wife was a slight woman and hadn't the weight to hold a determined half-grown pointer intent on leaving the showground. As I grabbed hold of the leash and hauled her to a halt, it emerged that, wandering on ahead, Cathy had been close to the clay pigeon shooting area just when the guns opened up. Fliss was having none of it; built like a small tank, she had taken off in panic.

We never did cure her of her fear of loud noises, and later had to replace the entire interior of various cars when Fliss might have been left peacefully within them in some distant car park, subsequently to become aware of distant thunder or gunfire. We would always hurry back, but in her panic to escape she would have demolished half the interior trim. But, if never destined to be a working dog, she was a superb family pet, loving and gentle (or as gentle as it is possible for a very large and very clumsy, tank-like lump of solid muscle to be). We sold a lot of cars without ceiling padding or with no interior trim on the rear doors.

It seems that many of our dogs are somehow damaged goods by the time we get them, and not in ways where I may take responsibility. The mongrel terrier – a hairy Border-Lakeland cross, with a few other varieties thrown in – had come from a well-respected line of working terriers in Assynt away to the north (when working at Inchnadamph

I had admired the mother enormously, and the keeper had kindly kept me a pup from the next litter). Although acquired as a pet for the children (who had always wanted a smaller dog to torment), it was clear that she too could never have been worked, since at a few weeks old she developed fits. With increasing frequency, whether at rest overnight, or actively running around the field during the day – there seemed no pattern to it – she would collapse on her side stiffening rigidly in catatonic seizures. She seemed to grow out of it in time – indeed is beside me as I write this, demanding attention as only a scrabbling terrier knows how – but only after some years, by which time she might well have been dead if she had collapsed with such a seizure away on the hill or trapped down a fox's earth

Like the others, though, the terrier loved these excursions to the beach, rushing along the shore barking cheerfully at nothing in particular. This part of Mull is a rather curious mixture: Calgary Bay, just a short distance along the coast, is a serious tourist trap for its similarly extensive white coral sands – and Calgary itself boasts one of these art-in-nature exhibitions, where a short woodland walk introduces the visitor to a series of al fresco sculptures. Nearby Dervaig, too, has much directed towards the tourist, while Tobermory of course has now become well known as the setting for the televised children's series Balamory. Yet hidden amongst these more blatant and brash attractions are still the peaceful places if you know where to look (well, peaceful until we arrive with our barking dogs; but we tend to favour unfrequented beaches). In my early days back in the Highlands, I used to visit Mull quite regularly because, as a supplement to our income, I had run a series of evening classes in Craignure and out at Pennyghael on the junction of this West Coast road and the long peninsula of the Ross of Mull; in consequence, I had come to know the island well. Mull's maze of largely single-track roads are something of a challenge, twisting and turning through the island – and the speed with which the locals, especially, travel is very evident from the number of battered wings and dented radiators of the island cars; but while I tend to avoid the more obvious tourist areas, I like the island and its people, especially this western coast and the leisurely pull out along the Ross of Mull to Bunessan, Fionnphort and Iona.

And today we were here with explicit purpose; for it was at Gruline that, supposedly, the eagerly expected solar eclipse was likely to be most complete and most visible. As on so many astronomical occasions before and since, the cloud was building and threatening to obscure the sun more effectively than any passing moon, but we urged children and canines into the truck and headed back along the road. In the event, we were lucky and actually had a reasonably clear view as the sky grew towards an artificial twilight and the air cooled. And if the dogs were not particularly impressed, the children at least grunted some scant acknowledgement before, like the dogs, returning to their slumbers in the rear seats. Oh well; some you lose. As the shadow passed and the day grew light again I drove my sleeping cargo back towards the ferry port of Fishnish.

YEAR'S END

Each year, as in many other small and tight-knit communities all over, the village put on a Christmas party. While each of us in the village was to a large extent self-reliant, life for all of us was equally to some degree intertwined with those of our neighbours and indeed interdependent with them. While we did not live entirely in each other's pockets, we depended on each other for assistance at lambing or clipping, for help with jobs like fencing or walling; we depended on each other, too, for social interaction and simple human encounter. We knew each other well; we worked together, and played together when time permitted. And the Christmas party (which might be held on any Saturday between Christmas itself and the second week of January) was one more way in which we might all come together when all the winter chores were done.

Everybody contributed and everybody attended, but it was especially geared towards the older folk, with entertainments and presents for the pensioners and any visiting children. (Although Lochuisge had few children of its own and the majority of folk were in their sixties or older, many had grandchildren visiting over the holiday period, who were more than welcome at the party.)

The hall had to be cleared and swept clean. Men with ladders were entreated to come and hang decorations from the tall windows or drape elderly paper chains and tinselled ropes from end to end across the high ceilings. A tree was 'borrowed' from the forestry (or at best donated by the Laird from his own commercial woodlands). While male assistance was sought (with ladders again) to entwine the fairy lights, we were then shooed away, for dressing the huge tree was women's work.

All who could cook were dragooned into preparing food for the buffet. That makes it sound as if there was an element of coercion, but in truth all were only too happy to contribute; it was merely a matter of organising those efforts and contributions into some coherent menu rather than have a simple surfeit of fruit salads or meringues. On the day itself we set up the little card tables of the whist drives with cheerful gingham cloths. Relays of folk ferried vast platters of sausage rolls, chicken drumsticks, plates of thin sliced lamb or venison, potato salads, pasta salads and hundredweights (it seemed) of boiled potatoes down to the hall, together with deep glass bowls of desserts: trifles, meringues, pavlovas, chocolate cake; the ladies of Lochuisge could all cook superbly, and the long trestle tables at the far end of the hall groaned under the weight.

And then the guests arrived. For most events in Lochuisge one could count on the earliest arrivals turning up at least an hour after the appointed time, but for the Party everyone was very prompt.

In truth, with such a relatively small community it was all a bit like a big family party; the assembling company was such a mixture, too: local crofters and shepherds, the Laird himself and the doctor and the Minister came visiting from Kinlochbuidhe as well as Lochuisge's own old folk. And there was such an eclectic range in age too: from the one-year-old baby of the new shepherd on Lochuisge to Seonaid and Kirsty's mama, still spry at 90 – and all ages in between. As ever, Niall the tractor had brought his box[28] and accompanied proceedings with a fine array of tunes. He was actually a very shy lad, and one increasingly got the impression that hiding behind his box and playing was the only way he had the confidence to join in on such occasions: providing the music gave him a role and a reason to do so.

The older folk were ushered to seats at the little card tables, while more able-bodied collected plates of victuals from the end table and brought it to them, only then returning to the main table to collect

---

28 piano accordian

platefuls for themselves. There were urns of tea and fruit squash – but no alcohol was served.

It must have seemed slightly odd to the older members of the community, who had after all, sat in this same room as their schoolroom many years before – all but Seonaid and Kirsty's mum, who had, if you will remember, come to Allt na Mhuillin many years before as a lady's maid and married a local lad. The buzz of contented chatter rumbled around the gentle strains of Niall's accordion until all had had enough to eat and drink. Tables were cleared and chairs pushed to the side walls of the hall, and we all played Pass the Parcel, then the children played Musical Chairs.

Time for Putman to leave for a while.

Outside in the shelter of the toilet block I climbed into the scarlet trousers and coat, stuffing a pillow down the front of the jacket and masking my face with an uncomfortably ticklish white beard. I topped it off with the requisite red hat, gathered the hessian sack of gaily-wrapped gifts, and made my way round to the front door of the hall. I hammered on the door; all went quiet within and the door was thrown open into the night. This year there were only half a dozen children amongst us, but the pensioners, too, would get a gift – a bottle of sherry for the women and whisky for the men. I felt a total fraud and suspected that even most of the children could recognise me behind the beard and the false frivolity, but nobody seemed to care. Playing Santa was normally Brian's job, but he happened to be away in the south this year and could not oblige, so I had been drafted in for the occasion. With a jingling of bells from outside (I still don't know who engineered that), Santa left for his reindeer sleigh; the younger children were gathered up and shooed home to bed, the real oldies were shepherded to seats around the edge of the hall, and Niall shouldered his accordion ready to lead us off into the first dance of the evening.

We might do a few formal country dances (after all, we had been rehearsing every Tuesday) but for the most part – and in order to include as many as possible – the bulk were traditional céilidh dances like the Dashing White Sergeant, the Gay Gordons, or Strip the Willow, even extending to somewhat shambolic Eightsome reels (shambolic because only half those present ever remembered the steps) – and with a few 'joined up dances' for good measure like St Bernard's Waltz or a Highland schottische. Sometimes we danced to taped music, sometimes we had a live band, but always there was Niall, too, to rely upon.

What was so special about it was that everyone danced with everyone else regardless of rank or marital status; this was our Party and for a moment we were all one extended family, and any temporary differences, such as must arise in any close-knit community, forgotten. This inclusiveness was a feature of all dances at Lochuisge. No one was left out – and indeed the better dancers went out of their way to include those less confident. I remember myself that, on one occasion when I had travelled up on my own to make some necessary arrangements before we made the final move, that visit coincided with the date of the summer (harvest) dance and there was no question but that I would have to attend. It had been many years since last I had done any formal (or even informal) Scottish dances, and initially I propped myself on the outskirts as a benevolent observer, although patently considerably younger than most of the other wallflowers. This wasn't to last, and it was only minutes before Netta (herself an 'outsider' but a regular holiday visitor from Fife, and a bonny dancer) swept me into the circle of stomping, shuffling, and sometimes nimble, feet to talk me back into the intricacies of a Britannia Two Step.

And the dancing went on, with only a short break for Niall to play a few Gaelic songs (which all joined in with gusto), until the stroke of midnight. (Well, the Minister was there, and it was a Saturday.) Magically, some of the ladies had been working behind the scenes, restoring order in the little kitchenette adjoining the main hall, and had cleared and washed up so that everyone could collect their now empty dishes and take them home again. Still humming the haunting strains of *Cailin mo rùin-sa* and with a cheerful chorus of *Oiche mhath* we all dispersed into the night. Lochuisge drew its curtains on another year.